MODERN RUSSIAN PROSE COMPOSITION BOOK ONE

MODERN RUSSIAN PROSE COMPOSITION

BOOK ONE (passages for translation into Russian—intermediate)
BOOK TWO (passages for translation into Russian—advanced)
MANUAL (MODERN RUSSIAN USAGE)

Modern
Russian Prose
Composition

BOOK ONE

PETER HENRY, M.A.

*Professor in the Department of Slavonic Languages
and Literature, University of Glasgow*

HODDER AND STOUGHTON
LONDON SYDNEY AUCKLAND TORONTO

ISBN 0 340 17479 X

First published 1963
Second edition: fifth impression 1979
Copyright © 1965 Peter Henry

Printed in Great Britain for
Hodder and Stoughton Educational,
a division of Hodder and Stoughton Ltd,
Mill Road, Dunton Green, Sevenoaks, Kent,
by Hazell Watson & Viney Ltd, Aylesbury, Bucks

Preface

This volume of annotated prose passages is intended primarily for students preparing for the Ordinary level General Certificate of Education and similar examinations. It is hoped that it may also prove useful for others who are proceeding from the elementary to the intermediate stage of the study of Russian.

The passages are arranged in order of increasing difficulty, the level of the last four or five being somewhat in excess of normal Ordinary level requirements. The subject matter is in the main practical, involving a basic vocabulary of some 1,200 words.

The grammatical and syntactical material contained in the passages is such as should normally be mastered by Ordinary level candidates. Gerunds and participles, the subjunctive, and declined numerals have been kept to a minimum.

Each passage is accompanied by Notes; these either give information on the spot, or refer the reader to a note elsewhere in the book, or give a paragraph number (e.g. §178). The numbers refer to the companion volume (*Manual of Modern Russian Prose Composition*) which is intended to be used in conjunction with this book. Some of the passages emphasise specific topics, in which case the Notes are prefaced by a reference to a particular section of the Manual to be studied, if desired, before the translation is attempted.

The author wishes to express his thanks to Professor Nadejda Gorodetzky, Professor of Russian, Liverpool University, who answered many questions on Russian usage; to the A.T.R. Textbook Committee, whose comments on an earlier version of the book were of great assistance; and to S. A. Khavronina of Friendship University, Moscow, who gave invaluable help with the use of specifically Soviet Russian terms and in many other ways.

In this second edition, a number of minor changes have been made and a few words have been added to the Vocabulary. The help of Mr Yury Vorobyov of Kiev University and Mrs E. L. Zuntz in preparing this edition is gratefully acknowledged.

P. H.

Acknowledgments

Grateful acknowledgment is due to the following Examination Boards for granting permission to reprint extracts from their examination papers:

Oxford and Cambridge Schools Examination Board (Passages 15, 17, 19, 22; Unannotated Passages II, V)

University of London University Entrance and Schools Examination Board (Passage 37; Unannotated Passage III)

University of Cambridge Local Examinations Syndicate (Unannotated Passages I, IV)

The author also expresses his gratitude to Messrs Hutchinson and Co. Ltd. for allowing him to include a slightly adapted excerpt from *Moscow, Sketches on the Russian Capital*, translated by Peggy Cochrane (Passage 36).

Contents

Abbreviations

acc.	accusative	*n.*	noun
adj.	adjective	*nom.*	nominative
adv.	adverb	*part.gen.*	partitive genitive
coll.	colloquial	*pfv.*	perfective
comp.	comparative	*pl., plur.*	plural
conj.	conjunction	*posn.*	position
dat.	dative	*p.p.p.*	past participle passive
dim.	diminutive	*prep.*	prepositional (locative)
emph.pron.	emphatic pronoun	*pres.*	present
f., fem.	feminine	*pron.*	pronoun
fut.	future	*prp.*	preposition
gen.	genitive	*refl.*	reflexive
g.pl.	genitive plural	*rel.*	relative
g.sg.	genitive singular	*sht.fm.*	short (predicative) form
indecl.	indeclinable	*sg., sing.*	singular
infin.	infinitive	*sup.*	superlative
instr.	instrumental	*tr.*	transitive
intr.	intransitive	*usu.*	usually
impfv.	imperfective	*vb.*	verb
m., masc.	masculine		
mtn.	motion (movement towards)		

8

1 My Room

When I was eleven[1] my parents gave me a room of my own.[2] They gave me the spare room upstairs. At first it was rather bare[3] but I soon made it very cosy.[3] I put my bed into the right-hand corner and my wardrobe behind the door. Mother gave me a little table with drawers and I put it in front of the window which looks out on to[4] the garden. Here I do my homework and write letters, etc.

She gave me two chairs and an old armchair as well.[5] Now, when my friends call on me, we can sit here and talk. The armchair usually stands in front of the fireplace and right under the lamp — a very good place[6] for reading. On the left of the fireplace is a chest of drawers; on the right a small bookcase where I keep my books. But I have so many that some lie on the chest of drawers and some even in the wardrobe. There are some[7] pictures on the wall that I chose myself.[8] Although the room is small[9] it is very comfortable[10] and I am very pleased with it.

NOTES

For translation of *to be*, see § 122 (i); of *there is/are*, see § 121; of *to put, lie, stand*, see § 136.

1. *when I was eleven*: see § 68.
2. *a room of my own*, **отде́льную ко́мнату.**
3. *it was rather bare, I . . . made it . . . cosy*: see §§ 44-45.
4. *looks out on to*: use **выходи́ть в/на** + *acc.*
5. *as well* (= *also, too*), **то́же, та́кже** and **и**; the last often expresses surprise. Note position: *Do you live here too?* **Вы то́же здесь живёте? И вы здесь живёте?** (i.e. in addition to all these others). *He is coming too*, **он то́же прихо́дит; и он прихо́дит.** Cf. *I, too, like music*, **я то́же люблю́ му́зыку;** *I like music as well* (in addition to my other interests), **я и му́зыку люблю́;** *I don't like it either*, **я то́же не люблю́ (её).**
6. *a very good place*: start with **э́то.**   7. *some*: omit; see § 81(iv).
8. *myself*: see § 76.   9. *is small*: see § 40.
10. *it is very comfortable*, **в ней о́чень удо́бно;** see § 137.

2 Our Town

I live in a small town[1] in the north of England. There is[2] a big castle in the centre of the town and several fine old churches. Here most of[3] the streets are dark and narrow; the houses stand in long rows[4] on both sides[5] of the streets and they are all very similar to each other. In the suburbs the houses are bigger[6] and newer[6] and the streets are wider.[6]

There are[2] three cinemas in the town. One of[7] them is not far from our house. I usually go[8] there once a week; but when a good play is on[9] we all go[8] to the theatre together. There are[2] five schools, one library and a museum. Before the war we still had trams, but now we only have buses. The railway station is outside the town.[10]

The town itself[11] is in no way[12] remarkable, but its surroundings are very pretty. There is[2] a little river[1] nearby, where one can bathe. On the other side of the river[13] there are some[14] low, green hills. We have already lived[15] here for eight years, and in my opinion this is a nice little town.[1]

NOTES

1. *a small town, etc.* Russian is very rich in diminutives and they are used extensively. It is quite common to use ма́ленький (itself a diminutive form) in conjunction with both diminutive adjectives and nouns: ма́ленький, хоро́шенький плато́чек; до́бренькая стару́шка, etc.
2. *There is, there are*: see §§ 14, 15, 121.
3. *most of.* Большинство́ is normally used of persons, бо́льшая часть, бо́льшей ча́стью of objects: большинство́ студе́нтов говори́ло свобо́дно по-англи́йски; бо́льшая часть го́рода была́ о́чень стара́; дома́ бо́льшей ча́стью бы́ли о́чень ста́рые.
4. *in long rows*: use *instr. pl.*
5. *on both sides*, по обе́им сторона́м or по о́бе сто́роны. (Note с обе́их сторо́н, *from both sides*; в о́бе сто́роны, *in both directions*.)
6. *bigger, newer, wider*: see §§ 49, 51.

7. *one of*: use из +*gen.*; see § 157 (vi).
8. *go*, see §§ 127-128.
9. *is on*, идёт; see § 133. Of films пока́зывать/показа́ть is also used: на про́шлой неде́ле шёл (пока́зывали) интере́сный фильм.
10. *outside the town*, за го́родом (за́ городом).
11. *itself*: see § 76.
12. *in no way*: here ниче́м.
13. *On the other side of the river*, за реко́й, на том берегу́ (реки́).
14. *some*: omit; see § 81 (iv).
15. *We have ... lived*: tense? see § 83.

3   My Family

Two years ago we moved into a new house in one of the suburbs[1] of London. It has[2] seven rooms: a sitting-room, dining-room and kitchen downstairs and[3] three bedrooms and a bathroom upstairs. There is[4] a little garden[5] behind the house.

We needed a bigger house, because for the past three years[6] our grandparents have been living[7] with us. It's much nicer here than in the old, cramped flat in town where we lived before. There is more room here, and, of course, we children like[8] playing in the garden very much.[9] On the other hand, we live further from the shops, theatres and cinemas. In town everything was much nearer.

My father works as an engineer in a big factory.[10] On Saturdays and Sundays[11] he works in the garden and we sometimes help him. My mother used to be a school-teacher,[12] but now she does not teach[13] any more, as she has plenty to do[14] in the house. I am thirteen years old[15] and go to a secondary school.[16] Mary is four years younger[17] than I and still goes to a primary school.[16] That's[18] our family.

NOTES

See §§ 49-53 on Comparatives. For transcription of English names, see § 201.

1. *in one of the suburbs*: see § 157 (vi). The phrase is still governed by the verb *moved* and is accordingly expressed by в + *acc.* Cf. мы пошли́ обе́дать в рестора́н, *we went to have dinner in the restaurant*; мы пое́хали в го́род в теа́тр, *we went to the theatre in town.*
2. *It has*: see § 183 (iii).
3. *and*: see § 165.
4. *There is*: see § 121.
5. *a little garden*: see passage 2, note 1.
6. *for the past three years*: see § 163 (iii).
7. *have been living*: tense? see § 83.
8. *like*: see § 186.
9. *very much*, о́чень; position? see § 16.
10. *works as an engineer*: see § 31; *in a big factory*: see § 153.
11. *On Saturdays and Sundays*: see § 162 (vi).
12. *used to be a school-teacher*: case? see § 27.
13. *teach*: use преподава́ть; see § 197.
14. *she has plenty to do*, у неё мно́го де́ла (not де́лать); она́ о́чень занята́.
15. *I am thirteen years old*: see § 68.
16. *go, goes to ... school*: see § 184.
17. *four years younger*: see §§ 69 (i), 70.
18. *That's*, вот (cf. French *voilà*).

4   A Conversation

A   Hullo, John, are you[1] going to town?
B   Yes, I am.[2] But unfortunately I have missed the bus and I'm afraid I shall be late for[3] work. I have to be[4] in the office by nine o'clock.

A   I always go by train. It leaves here at twenty past eight and arrives in town at ten to nine. It's a good train: it's hardly ever[5] late.

B   Good! I'll go with you. I don't like being late[6] for work and my boss doesn't like it either.[7] I usually get up at half past seven, but when I woke up today it was already after eight.

A   It's a pity we live so far from town, isn't it?[8] If we lived a little nearer[9] to the centre it would be much easier. By the way, where do you lunch?

B   Usually in a little restaurant near the station. I always go early, at a quarter to one, when there is[10] hardly anyone[5] there. If you like, we can have lunch there together.

A   All right. But we must[4] hurry, or else we shall miss the train as well.[7]

NOTES

See § 161 on Expressions of Time and §§ 127-9 on Verbs of Motion. For transcription of English names, see § 201.

1. *you*, ты (*sing.*, familiar form) and вы (*pl.* polite form). Ты and твой (твоя́, твоё, твой), *your*, are used when addressing small children, members of the family and close friends. It sounds very odd to address a small child as вы; the plural forms are used when several children are addressed.

2. *Yes, I am.* In this type of elliptical reply the word emphasised in the question (usually, but not necessarily, the verb) is repeated. «Вы бы́ли на конце́рте?» — «Был.» «Вы лю́бите му́зыку?» — «Люблю́.» «У вас большо́й дом?» — «Большо́й.»

3. *for*: see § 151 (iv).

4. *I have to be, must*: see § 189.

5. *hardly ever*, *hardly anyone*: translate 'almost never', 'almost no one'.

6. *like*: see § 186; *being late*: aspect? see § 100 (ii).

7. *not . . . either, as well*: see passage 1, note 5.

8. *isn't it?* не пра́вда ли? не так ли?

9. *If we lived*: see § 118; *a little nearer*: see § 53.

10. *is*: use быва́ть; see § 124.

5   *Letter from an English Schoolboy*

24th October, 1961

Dear Sergei,[1]

Our Russian teacher[2] was in the Soviet Union last year. He told us that some of[3] the Russian children[4] whom he met want to correspond with English children and gave me your address. That's why[5] I'm writing to you.

First I'll tell you a little about myself.[6] I am fourteen[7] and have two brothers and a sister. I am the eldest, and David, who is seven, is the youngest. At school we are learning two foreign languages,[8] French and Russian. They say that French is easier than Russian, but I don't know whether[9] this is true. For example, I think a French dictation is much harder than a Russian one.[10] But on the other hand, I must say that Russian grammar is very difficult indeed.[11] I like Chemistry best of all, and in my opinion the dullest subject is Mathematics. On Wednesdays and Saturdays we have games.[12] We play cricket in summer[13] and football in winter.

Do write to me, please, and tell me something[14] about yourself.[6] Tell me how many mistakes I have made in this letter. I hope not too many!

Best wishes,[15]

Jim

NOTES

See §§ 49-55 on Comparatives and Superlatives. For *you* and *your*, see passage 4, note 1. For transcription of English names, see § 201.

1. *Dear Sergei*, Дорогóй Сергéй! *Dear Sir* is Уважáемый (глубоко-уважáемый) товáрищ Иванóв (Сергéй Ивáнович, товáрищ редáктор, etc.).
2. *Russian teacher*, учи́тель (учи́тельница) ру́сского языкá. For word order of this sentence, see § 15.

14

3. *some of*: see § 157.
4. *children.* In many contexts **дети** and **ребята** are now interchangeable; but of a family only **дети** is used: **у них двое детей. Ребята** also means colloquially *young people, the boys*: **Я пошёл с ребятами на экскурсию. А что ребята делают?**
5. *That's why*, **вот почему.**
6. *about myself, yourself*: see § 78 (i).
7. *I am fourteen, etc.*: see § 68.
8. *we are learning*: see § 184; *two foreign languages*: see §§ 57, 58.
9. *whether*: see § 88.
10. *I think*: see § 172 (iv); *a French dictation is much harder than a Russian one* translate 'it is much harder to write a dictation in French (**на французском языке**) than in Russian'.
11. *I must say*, **надо сказать**; *Russian grammar is very difficult indeed*: translate 'is really very difficult'.
12. *we have games*: use **бывать**; see § 124.
13. *We play cricket in summer, etc.*: see § 154. For word order of this sentence, see § 15.
14. *something*: see § 80.
15. *Best wishes*, **С сердечным приветом** or **Всего хорошего!** More formally (=*yours sincerely*), **С искренним приветом,**

Уважающий Вас
Иван Петров.

6   *On the Way to Town (i)*

It was[1] a hot summer's day. Ivan Burov and his fourteen-year-old daughter were walking along the dusty road that leads from the village of Alexeyevka[2] to Kolomna. They were carrying a heavy suitcase and had already walked for over an hour, when they heard[3] the sound of an engine far behind them.[4] It was a lorry and although it was moving slowly, it was soon quite close. The driver was a young man of about twenty[5] with thick black hair and a jolly, suntanned face. 'Hullo,' he said.[6] 'Where are you going in such a terrible heat?' — 'What business is that of yours?'[7] Burov replied,[6] crossly. But after a pause[8] he added: 'To town, as you can see.[9] I am taking Tanya there. She is going[10] into Form Eight this year and there is only a seven-year school in our village. She will be staying[11] with my sister in town.' — 'If you like, I'll give you a lift,' said the driver. Burov looked at his daughter. She[12] laughed, nodded her head, and soon they were travelling in the noisy old vehicle. In it there were lots of wooden boxes, bundles and sacks, and very little room for passengers. But in any case, this was much better than going on foot.

NOTES

For Verbs of Motion in this and the following passage, see §§ 127-133; for translation of *his, her*, etc., §§46-48; for Prepositions, §§151-159, 162-163.

1. *It was*: see § 74 (ii).
2. *the village of Alexeyevka*, **село Алексéевка**; see § 32.
3. *they heard*: see § 95 (ii).
4. *behind them*: see § 78 (i).
5. *of about twenty*: see §§ 62, 69 (i).
6. *he said, etc.*: see § 18.
7. *What business is that of yours?* **А вам какóе дéло?**
8. *after a pause*, **помолчáв**, lit. *having kept silent for a while*, or **не срáзу,** *not at once*.
9. *as you can see*: translate 'as you see'. The complaint to the person sitting in front of you in the cinema «Я не могý вúдеть» could earn the retort «Зачéм тогдá вы хóдите в кинó?» Вúден (-нá, -но, -ны) is also commonly used: отсюда вúден весь гóрод, *you can see the whole town from here*; ничегó нé было вúдно, *one could not see anything*. Similarly я не слы́шу, не слы́шно, *I can't hear*.
10. *is going*: here пойдёт (*fut. pfv.* 'will go', 'will start going').
11. *will be staying*: see § 194.
12. *She*, **та** (rather than **онá**). **Тот, та, то, те**, emphasises the change of subject and shows that attention is now focused on a person previously mentioned in a subordinate sense. E.g. **Наконéц Илья́ Петрóвич обратúлся к Попóву, сидéвшему у окнá. Но и тот не слу́шал егó.**

16

7   On the Way to Town (ii)

'But tell me,' the driver asked, 'why didn't you take the bus?' 'Well, you know[1] that buses don't run every day[2] and Tanya must be there before the first of September, when the new school year starts. So, as there is no bus, we have to[3] walk,' Burov answered. The driver said that he was taking[4] fruit and vegetables to the market,[5] apples, pears, tomatoes and potatoes. 'I don't often go[2] to Kolomna. Usually I take all this to Voskresensk. I went there last Tuesday. But as it was raining and there was hardly anybody[6] on the market,[5] we didn't manage to sell everything[7] we had brought. That's why[8] I am going to Kolomna today.' — 'We are lucky,' Burov said with a laugh.[9] All the way the driver talked about his work, his small house, his family and about the weather. But Tanya was not listening to him. She was looking out of the window and thinking about her new life in town and about the new school. 'What will it be like?'[10] she asked herself and looked at her father. But he[11] was talking to the driver and did not notice her anxious look.

NOTES

1. *Well, you know,* вы же зна́ете.
2. *don't run every day, I don't often go*: for position of не, see § 146.
3. *have to*: see § 189.
4. *he was taking*: see § 87.
5. *to the market, on the market*: see § 153.
6. *hardly anybody*: see passage 4, note 5.
7. *everything*: case? see § 142.
8. *That's why*: see passage 5, note 5.
9. *said with a laugh,* засмея́лся; similarly вздохну́л, *said with a sigh*; удиви́лся, *said with surprise*.
10. *What will it be like?* Как э́то бу́дет?
11. *he*: see passage 6, note 12.

8   A Day in Town

Last Friday my brother and I[1] went to town. We left home at about three o'clock[2] and hoped we would have time[3] to do some shopping and then go to the theatre. Luckily the bus arrived soon; we went upstairs[4] and sat on the front seat.[5] I like sitting there because you have a good view[6] from there. There were many cars on the road and more and more people got on[7] the bus. Soon all the seats were taken.

We left the bus at the city centre. My mother wanted me to buy myself[8] some handkerchiefs, a white shirt and a pair of socks. Therefore I went into a large new department store, while John went to the library to change his book. Afterwards we met[9] at a small restaurant near the theatre, where we had tea. A new French play was on,[10] which we both wanted to see. We managed to get[11] tickets for two good seats[12] which were not too expensive.[13] The play was interesting[14] and we enjoyed it very much.[15]

When we returned it was already late. As we were very tired we went to bed at once.

NOTES

For Verbs of Motion, see §§ 127-135; for Word Order, §§ 13-16.

1. *my brother and I*: see § 158 (ii).
2. *left home*: use **выходи́ть/вы́йти из дому**; see § 22 (iii); *at about three o'clock*: see § 62.
3. *would have time*: tense? see § 87.
4. *we went upstairs*: use **поднима́ться/подня́ться наве́рх**.
5. *on the front seat*: use *pl.*; for case see § 136 (ii).
6. *you have a good view*, **хорошо́ ви́дно**.
7. *got on*: aspect? see § 91.
8. *wanted me to buy myself*: see §§ 78 (i), 115 (iii).
9. *we met*: see § 103 (ii).
10. *was on*: see § 133.
11. *to get*: see § 181.

12. *for two good seats*: see §§ 58, 151.
13. *were not too expensive*: use **стóить**, *cost.* Cf. **Э́тот костю́м стóил óчень дóрого,** *this suit was very expensive.*
14. *interesting*: see § 40.
15. *enjoyed it very much*: see §§ 16, 178.

9   Letter from Yury

Smolensk, U.S.S.R.
Ulitsa Lenina, House 4, Flat 11
23rd November, 1960

Dear John,

Many thanks for[1] your interesting letter. I showed it to our English teacher. She read it to us aloud, but I am afraid[2] it was rather difficult for us to understand everything you wrote. We only started learning English this year. I liked the stamps with the portrait of your Queen very much, but some of the boys say that our Soviet stamps, with pictures of historical monuments, portraits of writers, composers, artists and so on, are more interesting. If you like, whenever I write, I shall put[3] different stamps on the envelope. All right?

Last summer I spent six weeks[4] in a pioneer camp. We had a good time[5] there. The camp is near a river, and there is a big forest on the other side of it.[6] We saw many squirrels, rabbits and foxes there; but we didn't see any bears or wolves.[7] We did a lot of bathing, although I can't swim[8] yet, went for walks[9] and played volley-ball. Our team was very good[10] and we won quite often. But now we have to[11] work again.

When you write[12] again, please tell me about your school, about your holidays, about your friends — about everything.

Best wishes,
Yury

19

NOTES

See the Notes to passage 5.

1. *for*: see § 151.
2. *I am afraid*: here not meant literally, use к сожалению.
3. *whenever I write, I shall put*: for aspect and tense, see §§ 91, 117; use наклеивать/наклеить, *to stick on*.
4. *six weeks*, шесть недель or полтора месяца, *one and a half months*. Russians tend to reckon in months rather than weeks; similarly *six months*, полгода; *eighteen months*, полтора года.
5. *We had a good time*: see § 183.
6. *on the other side of it*: see passage 2, note 13.
7. *we didn't see any bears or wolves*: see §§ 142, 148.
8. *I can't swim*, мочь or уметь? see § 176 (i).
9. *went for walks*: see § 182.
10. *good*: here сильна, *strong*.
11. *we have to*: see § 189.
12. *When you write*: see §§ 91, 117.

10   Shops and Shoppers

My father has a grocer's shop. On Saturdays I help him there, because there are usually very many customers on that day.[1]

Father stands behind the counter and serves[2] those customers who want to buy sugar, butter, cheese, ham, tea and other groceries, which are kept[3] on the shelves behind him.[4] But vegetables — potatoes, cabbages, carrots, peas — and apples, pears, oranges and other fruit are kept[3] by the entrance. This is my place. The customers take their purchases from me,[5] but pay the money to Father.

It is sometimes amusing to watch the shoppers trying to decide
what to buy.[6] The women look at all the goods for a long time.
One of them asks what the eggs cost today.[7] She stands another
minute or two[8] and then goes out in order to compare our price
with the prices in other shops. She calls at the butcher's for some
meat,[9] at the baker's for bread and buns and then returns with her
baskets full[10] and buys a dozen eggs after all.[11] For women shopping is a serious business. Men, on the other hand, always like to
get their shopping done as quickly as possible[12] and are glad when
they manage to get what they want [13] or something like it,[14] right
away.[15]

NOTES

1. *there are usually*: see § 124; ... *on that day*: for word order, see § 15.
2. *serves*: use обслу́живать + *acc.*
3. *are kept*: use находи́ться or translate 'we keep'.
4. *behind him*, позади́ него́.
5. *from me*: see § 155 (ii).
6. *to watch the shoppers trying to decide*: see § 187; omit *trying to*,
   see § 94 (ii); *what to buy*: add им (*dat.* of они́), see § 150.
7. *what the eggs cost today*, ско́лько сто́ят сего́дня я́йца or по чём
   сего́дня я́йца.
8. *another minute or two*: see § 171.
9. *for some meat, etc.*: see §§ 81, 151.
10. *with her baskets full*: translate 'with full baskets'.
11. *a dozen eggs*: although the word дю́жина exists, it is more common to
    say деся́ток (*ten*); *after all*: position? see § 16.
12. *like*: see § 186; *to get their shopping done*: aspect? see §§ 91, 96; *as
    quickly as possible*: see § 179.
13. *manage to get*: aspect? see § 100 (ii); *what they want*, то, чего́ хотя́т
    or то, что им ну́жно.
14. *something like it*, что́-нибудь похо́жее.
15. *right away*: position? see § 16.

_11_   _At the Doctor's_

There are many people in the waiting room. There are women, who are sitting in their overcoats and scarves, and children who find it difficult to sit still[1] on their chairs. A grey-haired old man, who coughs all the time, is sitting in the corner. It is very close in the room, but it does not occur to anyone to open the window. Some people are looking at the old magazines that are lying on the low, round table in the middle of the room, others are just looking in front of them. Everyone is silent; obviously they have been awaiting their turn for a long time.[2]

When at last I go in to the doctor, he greets me with a tired voice[3] and asks me what is the matter with me.[4] I tell him that I don't feel too well,[5] have a headache and a bad cough.[6] He takes my temperature[7] and says: 'I think[8] you have a very heavy cold.[6] You had better[9] go home and go to bed.[10] 'And don't get up, or you'll get 'flu.[11] I'll give you some medicine for your cough[12] and I'll come and see you in two or three days.' I thank him and go out. 'Next, please!' I hear[13] behind me as I close the door. The poor doctor is very busy. It's as well[14] that he has not been taken ill himself.

NOTES

For Indirect Statement and Question, see §§ 87–89; for Word Order, §§ 14–16; for use of **сам** and **себя**, §§ 76, 78 (i).

1. _who find it difficult_: translate 'for whom (_dat._) it is difficult'; _to sit still_: see § 191.
2. _for a long time_: see §§ 84, 85.
3. _with a tired voice_: see § 158.
4. _what is the matter with me_, **чем я бо́лен**.
5. _I don't feel too well_: see § 180; for _not too well_ use **нева́жно**.
6. _a bad cough, a heavy cold_, **си́льный ка́шель, си́льная просту́да**.

22

7. *he takes my temperature*: see §§ 48, 196.

8. *I think*: see § 172 (iv).

9. *You had better*, вы лу́чше followed by the imperative. Cf. (Ты) лу́чше не ходи́ туда́! Лу́чше не спра́шивай. Пойдём лу́чше домо́й. See also § 115 (ii).

10. *go to bed*: use ложи́ться/лечь в посте́ль; see § 136 (ii).

11. *you'll get 'flu*, у вас бу́дет грипп.

12. *for your cough*: use от +*gen*.; see § 151.

13. *I hear*: here слы́шно.

14. *It's as well*, хорошо́.

12   On the Train *На поезде*

иностранцы

в английч поезда   *некогда не*

Foreigners often say that in English trains people never speak to each other. But this, of course, is not true. *Но это конечно не правда.*

не давно Not long ago I travelled to London. In my compartment there were many passengers and they talked to each other almost all the *почти* time. They told each other where they lived, where they were going,[1] *ехали и* and talked about the weather. As soon as the train started, a little *двигать в* girl, sitting[2] by the window, called out: 'We're off!'[3] I found out *они поехали* that she was going to her aunt's in Chiswick.[4] — 'It's somewhere[5] *мало* near the Thames but I don't know exactly where ...' 'Chiswick? That's easy to find. You[6] can get to it on the Tube. I'll show you where to go when we arrive,'[7] I told her. *Ведь*   *опасно*

'Goodness, how fast the train is going! Surely it's dangerous!' said an elderly lady. 'Do they go[8] so fast in foggy weather and at *туман-fog* *почу* night?' Her neighbour smiled, took out a book and began to read.[9] Here was a typical Englishman: during the whole journey[10] he did *типичный* not say a single word.[11] But as we arrived in London, he got up, and turning[2] to the lady he said with a strong accent:[12] 'Excuse me, I do not understand English. I am from[13] Poland.'

23

NOTES

For Verbs of Motion, see §§ 127-135; for translation of *say, talk, tell, etc.*, § 192; for transcription of English names, see § 201.

1. *where they lived, where they were going*: tense? see § 87.
2. *sitting, turning*: participle or gerund? see §§ 105, 112.
3. *We're off!* Поéхали! or Éдем!
4. *in Chiswick*: see passage 3, note 1.   5. *somewhere*: see §§ 79, 80.
6. *You*: see passage 4, note 1.   7. *when we arrive*: tense? see § 117.
8. *Do they go . . . ?* see § 19 (ii).   9. *began to read*: see § 100 (ii).
10. *during the whole journey*: see § 164.
11. *not a single word*: see §§ 56, 142.
12. *with a strong accent*: see § 158.   13. *from*: see § 152.

13   The Seasons

Winter in England is, as a rule, a dreary time. Although many people[1] dream[2] of a 'White Christmas', in fact it rarely snows[3] in December. The coldest months are January and February. The weather is usually damp and foggy; a cold wind blows from the sea[4] and it rains frequently. Although the temperature is rarely below freezing point,[5] even Russians say that they feel colder[6] here than in Russia, because the Russian climate is much drier than ours. They have[7] a severe winter with frost,[8] snowstorms and snowdrifts. People wear warm winter coats. The air is fresh and clear and one can go skating, skiing and sledging.[9] In a word, winter is the favourite season of many Russians.[10]

I like spring best of all. The days become longer and warmer, some flowers appear in the garden and the first green leaves can be seen[11] on the trees.

In summer it is pleasant to be out in the open, to swim, play tennis or cricket and go for trips into the country.

But soon autumn comes.[12] The leaves change colour and finally fall from the trees. The days become shorter, the weather worse and worse,[13] and we watch[14] the birds fly away to warmer countries.

24

NOTES

See §§49-55 on Comparatives and Superlatives.

1. *many people*: see § 60 (ii).
2. *dream*. A dream experienced during sleep is **сон, сновидéние**, verb **вúдеть во сне, мне снúтся**. **Мечтá, мечтáть** refer to daydreams.
3. *it rarely snows*: use **бывáть**; see § 124.
4. *from the sea*: for position, see § 15; for preposition, see § 153.
5. *below freezing point*, **нúже нулú**, *below zero* (based on centigrade; technically **тóчка замерзáния**).
6. *they feel colder*: see § 137.
7. *they have*: use **бывáть**; see § 124.
8. *with frost*: use *pl*.
9. *go skating, skiing, sledging*: see § 182.
10. *winter is the favourite season of many Russians*: translate 'for many Russians winter is the favourite season'; see § 60 (ii).
11. *can be seen*: translate 'we see' or 'are visible'. Cf. passage 6, note 9.
12. *autumn comes*: use **наступáть/-úть**.
13. *worse and worse*, **всё хýже**.
14. *we watch*: see § 187.

14   Summer Holidays[1]

ранне   *делать планы на лето*

In winter and early spring, people begin making plans for the summer. They carefully read the advertisements in the papers and look at bright posters of[2] ideal holiday resorts. There is a large choice and it is often hard to decide where to go. Most Englishmen take their holidays in summer; some choose something new every year, but others go to the same place[3] year after year. They take their children with them and, as a family, go to one of the numerous seaside resorts for[4] two or three weeks. The older people,[5] as a rule, *мало* merely sit in the sun[6] and relax, while the younger ones[5] play on the beach and bathe in the sea. The trouble is that most holidaymakers[1] go to the resorts at the same time,[3] during the school holidays, so that there is always a great crowd[7] everywhere: on the trains, in the hotels, in the restaurants and on the beach. In the most popular resorts there are sometimes[8] so many holidaymakers that you can scarcely see the sea.[9]

These seaside holidays have become traditional[10] for the British.[11] However, lately, more and more people have been spending[12] their holidays abroad.

NOTES

1. *holidays, holidaymakers, etc.* **Кани́кулы** are school and university holidays. **О́тпуск**, orig. 'leave of absence', has an official colouring: **ежего́дный о́тпуск**, *annual holiday*. **Пра́здник**, religious in origin, is now used for public holidays generally: **в СССР Пе́рвое ма́я — вели́кий пра́здник**; also contrast with **бу́дни**, *weekdays*: **по пра́здникам магази́ны закры́ты**. **О́тдых** (lit. *rest*), **отдыха́ть, отдыха́ющие**, are now used for *holiday, be on holiday* or *spend one's spare time, holidaymakers*. **Брат отдыха́ет в Крыму́**; **мы ча́сто отдыха́ем за́ городом**; **отдыха́ющие е́дут на юг**. **Дом о́тдыха**, *holiday centre, rest home*; **выходно́й день**, *day off*.
2. *of*: use here **изобража́ющие**, *depicting*.
3. *the same place, the same time*: see § 77.
4. *for*: see § 163.
5. *The older people, the younger ones*: translate 'the old', 'the young'.
6. *in the sun*: see § 154.
7. *a great crowd*, **мно́го наро́ду**; see § 22 (i).
8. *are sometimes*: see § 124.
9. *you can scarcely see the sea*: see passage 4, note 5 and passage 6, note 9.
10. *traditional*: case? see § 45.
11. *the British*: use **англича́не**; similarly **А́нглия** is normally used for *Great Britain* (officially **Великобрита́ния**).
12. *more and more people*: see passage 13, note 13; *have been spending*: tense? see § 83.

26

15 A Walk in the Country[1]

One day some boys were walking in a wood. It was a long way from the town[2] where they lived and they did not go there often. In the wood was a castle, which they wanted to visit. They had left the town early — at eight o'clock. They first went by bus, then got out and began walking. They had brought[3] some lunch: bread and cheese and apples,[4] and one boy had a bottle of lemonade. It was a fine day and it was pleasant walking through the trees.[5] After some time they stopped and ate their lunch. After lunch they sat under a tree and talked about their walk. The castle was quite near now, but they had to be there in time to meet their teacher. He had promised to show them the castle and tell them about its history. He knew a great deal about the place[6] — more than anyone else[7] — and hoped to write a book about it. The oldest boy had a watch; after a few minutes he looked at it and said: 'Are we[8] all ready? It is time for us[8] to go.' All the boys stood up, and they set off once more.

(*Oxford and Cambridge Schools Examination Board, July 1960*)

NOTES

For Verbs of Motion see §§ 127-135.

1. *A walk in the country*, прогу́лка за́ город.
2. *from the town*: translate 'from that town'.
3. *had brought*: use брать/взять с собо́й. Cf. § 78 (i).
4. *some lunch*: *bread and cheese and apples*: see §§ 22 (i), 81.
5. *through the trees*: translate 'under the trees'.
6. *about the place*: translate 'about this place'.
7. *more than anyone else*: see § 54.
8. *we, for us*: omit.

16   A Summer's Day

It is a beautiful summer's day. The sun is shining brightly,[1] the sky is blue and a gentle breeze is blowing. We are sitting in the garden drinking coffee.[2] High above us we can hear the birds singing.[3] The roses are in full bloom. It is good just to sit and enjoy[4] the wonderful weather and breathe the fresh, pure air.

The children come running into[5] the garden. 'Come and see what we've found on the river!' they shout. We do not feel much like[6] getting up but in the end we do[7] and go with them into the little wood at the bottom of our garden.[8] It is cool and quiet here; only the wind is rustling gently in the leaves. Suddenly a little squirrel runs across our path and vanishes in some thick shrubs. We come out of the wood and see the river before us. The children are playing in an old boat which is lying by the river bank. 'This is what[9] we found!' they say proudly. 'We want to go boating.'[10] But as we come a little closer,[11] we see a hole in the bottom of the boat. 'Better not,' I say, 'none of you can swim.'[13]

NOTES

Particular attention should be paid to Word Order (see §§ 13-16).

1. *The sun is shining brightly*: translate 'a bright sun is shining'.
2. *drinking coffee*: translate 'and are drinking coffee'.
3. *High above us*: see § 78 (i); *we can hear the birds singing*: see § 89.
4. *enjoy*: see § 178.
5. *come running into*: translate 'run into'.
6. *We do not feel much like*: see § 180.
7. *we do*: supply 'get up'.
8. *at the bottom of our garden*: use за + *instr.*
9. *This is what*, вот что.
10. *go boating*: see § 182.
11. *come a little closer*: use подходи́ть/подойти́; see § 53.
12. *can swim*: see § 176 (i).

17   Our New House

We have recently bought a new house. It is in the country,[1] a few miles from the town[2] where we have been living. Our house in the town was old and rather small. It was situated[1] in one of the main streets. All day cars and buses were going by and it was very noisy. Sometimes at night it was difficult to sleep because of the noise. Our new house was only built[3] last year. It is much bigger than the old one — it has[4] four large rooms downstairs, and five bedrooms on the first floor. One of the rooms downstairs is a sitting-room, and this has[4] a very large window, from which one can see[5] the garden and the wood. We do not need[6] all the bedrooms, but perhaps our friends will visit us[7] and they can sleep there. We hope that they will come often in the summer, for they are very fond of the country. We can play tennis[8] in the garden and have walks in the fields, and not far away is a river where we can bathe. We have been living[9] in our new house only three weeks, but we like it very much already: it is so quiet and clean after the town.[10]

(*Oxford and Cambridge Schools Examination Board, July 1961*)

NOTES

1. *It is, was situated*: see § 122 (i); *in the country*: here в предместье.
2. *a few miles from the town*: see §§ 60 (ii), 73.
3. *was only built*: see §§ 108-110.
4. *it has, this has*: see § 183.
5. *from which*, в которое (lit. 'through which'); *one can see*: see passage 6, note 9.
6. *We do not need*: see § 189.
7. *will visit us*: aspect? see § 91.
8. *play tennis*: see § 154.
9. *We have been living*: tense? see § 83.
10. *after the town*: position? see § 15.

18   A Holiday Abroad

Our plane was due to leave London Airport early in the morning on the fifth of August and therefore we travelled to London on the previous day and spent the night in an hotel. We children were so excited that we could not fall asleep for a long time. The next morning we woke up very early. We had brought very little luggage with us;[1] we packed everything quickly and left the hotel. Father took the tickets and passports, and Peter and I a suitcase each.[2]

We were told[3] that our plane was[4] one of the latest and most comfortable in the world. I do not know whether[5] this is true, but in any case it was much bigger than I had expected. The aeroplane took off and soon we were flying high above the earth, and we could see[6] England and France beneath us,[1] as on a map. Two hours later we landed in Geneva.

We spent two wonderful weeks[7] in the mountains. It only rained once, on the return journey, when we were already over England again. We all agreed that this holiday had been very interesting and enjoyable. As for me,[8] I liked the aeroplane trip best of all.

NOTES

For Comparatives and Superlatives, see §§ 49-55; for transcription of English names, see § 201.

1. *with us, beneath us*: see § 78 (i).
2. *a suitcase each*: see § 64.
3. *We were told*: see §§ 111, 139.
4. *that our plane was*: for tense, see § 87.
5. *whether*: see § 88.
6. *we could see*: see passage 6, note 9.
7. *two wonderful weeks*: see § 58.
8. *As for me*, что касается меня.

I was ill a little while ago and had to lie in bed for a whole week.[1]
I read quite a lot, but after the second day I got bored.[2] I could
look out of the window,[3] but there was not much to see.[4] I could
hear the children playing in the street,[5] and sometimes people talked
under my window. My mother was very busy all the time, and I only
saw her when she brought[6] my breakfast and dinner. On Monday
I received a letter from a friend. He wrote[7] that he was coming to
see me that day.[8] I was very glad and impatiently waited for him
to come.[9] He came at eleven o'clock. First we talked about my
illness; then he told me about all[10] he had been doing. He looked
at my books, and asked if they were interesting. He had dinner[11]
with me and we talked about school and our friends. He went away,
but soon came back; he brought me two books and some apples,
which he had just bought. When at last he went home I was tired,
but felt much happier.[12] I knew I would soon be better.[13]

(*Oxford and Cambridge Schools Examination Board, July 1958*)

NOTES

For Indirect Statement and Question, see § 87-89.

1. *had to lie in bed*: see § 189; *for a whole week*: see § 163.
2. *I got bored*: see § 137.   3. *out of the window*: see § 154.
4. *there was not much to see*: translate 'nothing interesting there'.
5. *I could hear the children playing*: see passage 6, note 9 and § 89; *in the
   street*: see § 153.
6. *when she brought*: aspect? see § 91.   7. *He wrote*: see § 97.
8. *that day*: for position, see § 15.
9. *waited for him to come*, ждал, когда́ он придёт.
10. *about all*, о всём том, что; see § 169.
11. *He had dinner*: see § 96.
12. *felt much happier*: translate 'felt more cheerful'; see §§ 137, 180.
13. *would soon be better*, скоро попра́влюсь.

20 A Journey to Russia

Two years ago we went to the Soviet Union. We had wanted to go for a long time,[1] and at last we had saved enough[2] money for the journey. We had a visa for four weeks and we went by train, through Holland, Germany and Poland. We travelled for three and a half days. In Berlin we changed trains and from there[3] travelled in a Russian train. We were in a very comfortable compartment for four persons,[4] and we were never crowded.[5] There was[6] a dining car in the train, and besides, whenever we asked him, the attendant would bring us some tea. We were given[7] blankets, pillows and sheets and in the evenings the whole carriage became[8] a sleeping car. Brest, situated right on[9] the Polish frontier, was the first Russian town[10] we saw. Here we waited for three whole hours, while they changed the carriage wheels. (In the U.S.S.R. the railway track is wider than in the West.[11])

We visited the three main cities: Moscow, the capital[12] of the U.S.S.R., Leningrad and Kiev. But we saw the Russian countryside too: huge, silent forests, endless steppes, broad rivers and picturesque villages. It was all very interesting and I would like[13] to go there again sometime.[14]

NOTES

For Verbs of Motion, see §§ 127-135; for Numerals, §§ 57-58, 61, 63; for translation of *for*, §§ 151, 163.

1. *for a long time*, давно́ ог до́лго? see §§ 84, 85.
2. *enough*, доста́точно + *gen.* Дово́льно means *enough* only when used on its own: «Нале́йте, пожа́луйста, ещё ча́ю . . . дово́льно!» (*enough, that will do*). Otherwise, when qualifying adjectives or adverbs, дово́льно means *fairly, rather, reasonably*. Contrast э́то дово́льно хорошо́, *this is fairly good*, and э́то доста́точно хорошо́, *this is good enough*.
3. *from there*: here да́льше.

4. *four persons*. Человéк (*pl.* лю́ди) means *human being, person*; муж-чи́на means *man* as opposed to же́нщина, *woman*. Thus, она́ о́чень интере́сный челове́к. Молодо́й челове́к is *young man*, as opposed to молода́я же́нщина, (молода́я) де́вушка. See also § 69 (ii).
5. *we were never crowded*: impersonal construction, see § 137.
6. *There was*: for word order, see §§ 14, 15.
7. *We were given*: see §§ 111, 139.
8. *became*: use превраща́ться/преврати́ться в + *acc.*, *be transformed into*.
9. *right on*: see § 77.
10. *the first Russian town*: case? see §§ 27, 28.
11. *in the West*: see § 153.
12. *the capital*: case? see § 32.
13. *I would like*: see § 115 (i).
14. *sometime*: see §§ 79, 80.

21   The Arrival

Ivan woke me up early in the morning. 'Wake up!¹ Have a look out of the window!'² he was saying. I climbed down from my bunk and looked out. There was a broad stretch of water in front of us; the bright morning sun was shining on it. 'What is this?' I asked. 'A big lake?' — 'No, that's the Volga,' Ivan said with a broad smile.³ 'It's time to get ready. We shall be in Saratov in half an hour.' We packed our things and got our tickets from the attendant.⁴ Soon we came into a large town and for a time lost sight of the river. When the train stopped we said good-bye to our fellow passengers and jumped down on to the platform.

Ivan's mother was there to meet us.⁵ She kissed her son and shook hands with me.⁶ 'I am very glad to meet you,' she said. 'Let's go home and have breakfast. It's all ready. Then you can go and have a look at the town.'

After breakfast Ivan said: 'Let's go down to the river straight away and have a swim.⁷ I'll show you the town another time.'⁸ We picked up our bathing costumes and off we went.

NOTES

Particular attention should be paid to Word Order (see §§ 13-16); for translation of *to be*, see §§ 120-122.

1. *wake up, etc.*: see passage 4, note 1.
2. *out of the window*: see § 154.
3. *with a broad smile*: see § 158.
4. *got our tickets*: see § 181; *from the attendant*: use y +*gen.*; see § 155 (ii).
5. *was there to meet us*, встречáла нас.
6. *and shook hands with me*, а мне пожáла рýку; cf. §§ 48, 165.
7. *have a swim*: see § 183.
8. *another time*: see § 154.

22   In the Park

One day when I was sitting on a bench in the park, reading a paper,[1] a man came up[2] and spoke to me. He was an old man, poorly dressed and unshaven.[3] He said he had once known[4] my father and had often visited us some years ago. Now he had lost his money, could not find work,[5] and had nowhere to live.[6] I put my paper on the bench and asked him to sit down. I looked at his face,[7] but could not remember[8] that I had seen him before. It was clear that he wanted some money,[9] but why did he say he knew my father? I decided to find out whether he was telling the truth. 'What is my name?'[10] I asked. He told me[10] at once. I was surprised at this, but thought that someone might have told him[11] who I was. Then I asked him another question. 'Where were we living when you last saw us?' — 'In the house by the church. I used to come on Sundays and sometimes we went on the river in a boat.'[12] When he said this, I suddenly remembered him. He was an old friend of the family, but how he had changed![13]   (*Adapted*)

(*Oxford and Cambridge Schools Examination Board, December 1959*)

NOTES

For Indirect Statement and Question, see §§ 87-89

1. *reading a paper*: see § 112.
2. *a man came up*: see § 14.
3. *poorly dressed and unshaven*: see §§ 43, 106.
4. *had once known*, когда́-то знал; cf. § 86.
5. *could not find work*: § 143.
6. *had nowhere to live*: see § 150.
7. *I looked at his face*: see § 48.
8. *could not remember*: subjunctive follows; see §115 (v). Вспомина́ть/ вспо́мнить, *remember, recall, reminisce*: мы сиде́ли в клу́бе и вспомина́ли ста́рые времена́ (о ста́рых времена́х), *we sat in the club and talked about old times*; поду́май хороше́нько, вспо́мни, *try to remember*. По́мнить/за– is less precise and conscious, *to remember, not forget*: всю жизнь бу́ду по́мнить (=не забу́ду) э́тот прекра́сный ве́чер. «Вы по́мните его́ а́дрес?» — «Нет, не по́мню (= забы́л).» A little later, however, he might say: «Я то́лько что вспо́мнил его́.»
9. *some money*: see § 81.
10. *What is my name? ... He told me*: see §175.
11. *might have told him*: see § 176 (ii).
12. *we went on the river in a boat*: see § 182.
13. *how he had changed!* see § 177.

23   *After School*[1]

'What happened to you?'[2] Stephen's mother exclaimed as he returned from school, an hour later[3] than usual. He was covered in mud[4] and there was blood on his knees.[5] 'Oh, nothing.[6] We were playing football and I fell on a sharp stone,' he answered quickly. His mother frowned. 'Just look at your trousers[5] and your shoes.

I told you more than once[7] to come home straight after school. Go into the bathroom and have a good wash.[8] And change your clothes!' she said angrily.

When Stephen came downstairs she was laying the table for tea. 'I'm sorry, Mother,' he said, showing her his jacket. There was a big hole in the sleeve. 'And that was your best jacket,' she said with a sigh. 'You've been fighting, haven't you?'[9] He nodded his head. 'With whom?' — 'Oh, no one.'[6] Mother put down the plate she was holding in her hand. 'In the first place[10] you spoil your clothes; in the second place,[10] you don't tell the truth; and now this stupid answer to my question. You had better[11] go to your room and stay there. You are not going to have tea with us.' He went out of the door quietly; he just could not tell her why[12] he had been fighting.

NOTES

For Word Order, see §§14, 18; for Gerunds, §112; for translation of *with*, §158; of *you*, *your*, see passage 4, note 1.

1. *After school*, **после занятий**.
2. *What happened to you?* See §158 (iii).
3. *an hour later*: see §70.
4. *He was covered in mud*: see §§25, 154.
5. *on his knees, look at your trousers*, etc.: see §48.
6. *Oh, nothing*, **да ничего**; *Oh, no one*: translate 'with no one'.
7. *more than once*: see §91.
8. *have a good wash*: use **как следует**; see §189 (v).
9. *haven't you?* **Да?**
10. *In the first (second) place*, **во-первых, во-вторых**.
11. *You had better*, **поди-ка ты лучше**.
12. *why*. **Почему** covers most shades of meaning; **зачем, для чего**, *with what purpose, what for*; **отчего**, *for what reason* (**по какой причине**). «**Зачем (почему) вы пришли?**» — «**Я (пришёл) за советом.**» «**Отчего (почему) вы не пришли вчера?**» — «**Я был болен.**»

24 At the Cinema

Last week my friend and I[1] went to the cinema. There was a new Russian film[2] which we both very much wanted to see.[3] We had to[4] queue for twenty minutes. Then we bought our tickets and went inside.[5]

The main film had just begun.[6] It was a film about the Russian Civil War. I thought it was rather good. It told of the love of a simple peasant girl,[7] a member[8] of a partisan detachment, and a young White Guard officer[7] whom she had taken prisoner. For some time they were alone on a deserted island in the Aral Sea in Central Asia. Here they stayed for several weeks, until[9] one day they sighted a boat. When it came close to the shore they saw that it was full of Whites. The officer ran out to the boat, but just at that moment the girl shot him dead. That was the end of the film. I had found it more difficult[10] to understand the dialogue than I had expected: the actors spoke too quickly. Besides, I could not follow the action[11] very well either.[12]

In the interval we had some ice-cream.[13] Then we saw the second film, which was rather dull. When we came out of the cinema it was already nine o'clock. My friend, who lives near the cinema, walked home;[14] I live further away[15] and so went home by bus.

NOTES

For Verbs of Motion see §§ 127-135.

1. *my friend and I*: see § 158.
2. *There was a new Russian film*: see passage 2, note 9 and § 133.
3. *to see*: see § 187.
4. *We had to*: see § 189.
5. *went inside*: translate 'entered'.
6. *had just begun*: see § 103 (iii).
7. *peasant girl, White Guard Officer*: see § 34.
8. *a member*: case? see § 32.
9. *until*, **покá ... нe**; see § 166.

10. *I had found it more difficult*: see passage 11, note 1.
11. *follow the action*: see § 187.
12. *not . . . either*: see passage 1, note 5.
13. *we had some ice-cream*: see §§ 81, 183.
14. *walked home*: add пешко́м, *on foot*.
15. *further away*: add 'from town' or 'from the cinema'.

25 *In a Restaurant*

Next morning[1] I went to have breakfast with my two Russian friends.[2] The dining-room was already quite full,[3] but we managed to find an empty table[4] by the window. 'I'll order breakfast in Russian,' I announced boldly. 'I hope they will understand me.' A waiter came up to us. 'Please[5] bring an omelette, some cold meat,[6] brown bread,[7] butter and cheese. I also want something to drink, but there is no glass here,' I added, using the wrong word.[8] The waiter did not understand. 'Do you want me to[9] close the window?' he asked. Gleb burst out laughing.[10] 'You mean[11] (drinking) glass!' I saw my mistake.

After breakfast we had a glass of tea each.[12] Gleb said to me: 'You ate[13] very little. Didn't you like[14] your breakfast?' — 'Yes, thanks, I did.[14] At first I did not like Russian cooking, but I have got used to it now and I like it very much.' — 'Time to go,' Volodya reminded us. 'We are to be at the Gorky Library at ten o'clock, so let's go quickly.'[15]

NOTES

1. *Next morning*: see § 190.
2. *with my two Russian friends*: see § 60 (i).
3. *The dining-room was . . . full*: translate 'in the dining-room there were already many people'; see § 22 (i).

4. *an empty table*, свобо́дный сто́лик.
5. *Please*. Пожа́луйста usually follows the imperative: Напиши́те, пожа́луйста, когда́ вы бу́дете в Москве́. Да́йте са́хар, пожа́луйста.
6. *some cold meat, etc.*: partitive genitive, see §§ 22, 81.
7. *brown bread*: translate 'black bread'.
8. *wrong word*: see § 200.
9. *Do you want me to*: see § 115 (iii).
10. *burst out laughing*: see § 95 (i).
11. *You mean*: see § 188.
12. *a glass of tea each*: see §§ 22, 64.
13. *You ate*. Есть and ку́шать. Ку́шать is used with вы, in invitations to meals, etc. «Ку́шайте, пожа́луйста, пиро́г.» «Ку́шайте, това́рищи, что (=отчего́) вы не ку́шаете?» Есть is used with 1st and 3rd pers.: я не ем суп; ребя́та е́ли с аппети́том; also 2nd pers. sing.: «Почему́ ты ничего́ не ел?»
14. *Didn't you like . . . ? etc.*: see §186; for aspect, see §94; *Yes . . . I did*: see §147.
15. *let's go*: see §185 (ii); *quickly*, скоре́е (*comp.*); see §53 (Note).

26 My Grandparents

My father's parents lived in the country near a large farm. I often visited them when I was small,[1] for I liked helping[2] to look after the animals on the farm. My grandparents were very kind to me, but I had to behave well and was not to[3] make a noise in the house or walk in muddy boots on the clean floors that Grandmother washed every day. On Sundays we went to church and spent the day very quietly. I had to sit and read a book of poems that Grandmother gave me, and I was not allowed to[3] run about the house or play in the garden, even when it was fine.[4]

In his youth Grandfather must have been very handsome. Now he was very old. He liked to sit[2] in a large armchair and smoke his pipe. He had a large gold watch on a chain and sometimes he showed me how it worked.[5] Grandmother was younger than he.[6] She always had plenty to do.[7] I remember[8] in the winter evenings she would sit[9] by the fire and tell me old fairy tales and stories about her childhood.[10] But even then she would be working,[9] either making a dress[11] for Mother or knitting thick winter socks for Grandfather and me.

NOTES

For the use of Aspects, see § 91; for *must, have to*, see § 189.

1. *when I was small*: see § 44.
2. *I liked helping, he liked to sit*: see § 186.
3. *was not (allowed) to*: see § 176 (ii).
4. *when it was fine*: see § 122 (i).
5. *how it worked*: tense? see § 89.
6. *younger than he*: see §§ 51, 52.
7. *had plenty to do*: see passage 3, note 14.
8. *I remember·* see passage 22, note 8; followed by как and subordinate clause.
9. *would sit, would be working*: see § 125, or use plain imperfectives.
10. *about her childhood*: see § 47.
11. *making a dress*: make into a main verb, using шить/с– плáтье.

27   A Game of Hide-and-Seek

On the very first evening of our summer holidays[1] we decided to have a game of hide-and-seek. My brothers and I were staying[2] with an old uncle of ours who lived in a lonely part of Cornwall.

Dusk was already falling[3] and we could hear an owl hooting somewhere in the trees.[4] It was my turn to look for the others. I counted up to sixty[5] and then called out:[6] 'I'm coming!' and ran towards the trees. I saw[7] a small figure behind some shrubs which I took to be[8] my youngest brother Arthur. I ran up to catch him, but found, to my surprise, that it was a little girl in a white frock. She looked at me with frightened eyes[9] and then turned[10] and ran down the path. 'Who are you? Where do you come from?'[11] I called, but she did not stop and soon disappeared in the dark.

I went back into the house. My uncle was sitting by a brightly burning fire reading the newspaper.[12] He looked at me with a barely perceptible smile[9] and then went on reading. Five minutes later the boys came in and asked what had happened to me.[13] I told them that I had completely forgotten about the game, and that anyway it was too dark to find anyone.[14]

NOTES

For Indirect Statement and Question, see §§ 87-89; for Verbs of Motion, §§ 127-135; for transcription of English names, § 201.

1. *On the very first evening*, в пе́рвый же ве́чер; *of our summer holidays*: see passage 14, note 1.
2. *were staying*: see § 194.
3. *Dusk was already falling*, уже́ смерка́лось; see § 137.
4. *we could hear*: see passage 6, note 9; *an owl hooting*: see § 89; *somewhere in the trees*: see § 79; for word order, see §§ 14, 15.
5. *up to sixty*: see § 57.
6. *called out*: see § 95 (i).
7. *I saw*: see § 95 (ii).
8. *took to be*: see § 196.
9. *with frightened eyes, with a barely perceptible smile*: see § 158.
10. *turned*: see § 198.
11. *Where do you come from?* Ты отку́да?
12. *reading the newspaper*: see § 112.
13. *what had happened to me*: see § 158.
14. *anyone*: see § 80.

28   A History Lesson[1]

It is 9 a.m. All the children are at their places. The first lesson is just beginning.[2] Mr. Smith, the History master,[3] enters the classroom. All the boys stand up and say 'Good morning!' to him. He replies and we sit down again. At first the teacher tests us on our homework.[4] We are studying the period of the French Revolution[5] of 1789. We are all interested in this and everybody answers well. Only Alan does not seem to know anything. To the question 'Who was Danton?' he answers that he was the most reliable adviser of the French king. Everybody laughs and the teacher makes him copy out the homework again. Then he tells us about the life of Napoleon, the brilliant general and statesman, under whom[6] France became the most powerful state in Europe. On the map he shows us all the countries which Napoleon conquered — Italy, Egypt, Spain, Austria, Prussia, etc. — and tells us how[7] he became the master of most of Europe, except England and Russia. We all listen attentively. But there goes the bell[8] — ten to ten, the end of the first lesson. It had been so interesting that we had not even noticed how quickly the time had passed.

NOTES

For *to become*, see §§ 31, 45; for Nouns in Apposition, § 32; for transcription of English names, § 201.

1. *History lesson*, уро́к исто́рии.
2. *is just beginning*: see § 103 (iii).
3. *the History master*: see passage 5, note 2.
4. *tests us on our homework*, спра́шивает уро́к.
5. *the French Revolution*: see § 5.
6. *under whom*: use при + *prep.*; see § 160.
7. *how*, о том, как; see § 169.
8. *there goes the bell*: use раздава́ться/разда́ться; see § 182.

42

29   Eileen Arrives at the Farm

The bus stopped and Eileen got off. 'The farm is ten minutes' walk from the bus stop.[1] You will pass a large field, in which you will see some cows and sheep. Turn left there.' Eileen knew the whole letter by heart. She set off along a road that led between fields and meadows towards a little copse. Soon she saw a herd of cows on her left. 'There are a lot of them,' she thought. 'I wonder[2] if they all belong to Mr. Jones?' There were no sheep, but she saw some calves standing under the trees.

The farm was bigger[3] than she had expected. It was a large stone house with a red roof. Around it stood a barn, a cowshed, stables and other buildings. She walked up to the house and knocked at the door. The farmer's wife met her with a friendly smile. 'I'm just going to feed the hens. Do you want to come with me?' she said. As they crossed the yard Eileen asked whether they had any horses.[4] 'Yes, we have,' Mrs. Jones answered. 'But we hardly ever use them for work in the fields. We have tractors for that.[5] — Can you ride?'[6] — 'No, but I would like to learn,'[7] Eileen answered.

NOTES

For Verbs of Motion, see §§ 127-135; for transcription of English names, see § 201.

1. *The farm is ten minutes' walk from the bus stop*: translate 'from the bus stop to the farm is a ten minute walk (де́сять мину́т ходьбы́).'
2. *I wonder*: see § 199.
3. *The farm was bigger*: see § 122 (ii).
4. *asked whether they had*: see § 88; *any horses*: see § 82.
5. *We have tractors for that*: for word order, see § 14.
6. *Can you ride?* see § 176 (i).
7. *I would like to learn*: see §§ 184, 186.

I go to a new secondary school.[1] It is a large two-storeyed building which stands on the outskirts of the town. From a distance it looks as if[2] the walls are made of glass;[3] in fact, one side of each classroom consists almost entirely of windows. Thus there are no dark corners,[4] as in the older schools.[5] On hot summer days we open all the windows wide and sometimes even have lessons in the open.[6] It is not cold in our classroom in winter; on the contrary, it is sometimes even too warm.

Our classroom is on the first floor.[7] Here we have most of our lessons.[8] But there are also special rooms,[9] like the Physics and Chemistry laboratories, the Music room and the Gym, which are used[10] by all classes. There is a good canteen in the school,[11] where we can have dinner. The food is very good and cheap.[12]

There are nearly five hundred pupils in the school; in my form there are thirty-four. In the summer we are taking the G.C.E. 'O' level examination.[13] This is an important examination and we have to work very hard.[14]

NOTES

For Word Order, see §§ 13-16.

1. *I go to a new secondary school*: see § 184.
2. *it looks as if*, ка́жется, как бу́дто.
3. *made of glass*: use стекля́нный.
4. *there are no dark corners*: see §§ 141, 148.
5. *the older schools*: translate 'the old schools'.
6. *have lessons*, уро́ки (заня́тия) веду́тся or прохо́дят; *in the open*: see § 154.
7. *on the first floor*: translate 'on the *second* floor'.
8. *most of our lessons*: see passage 2, note 3.
9. *special rooms*, специа́льные кабине́ты (спецкабине́ты).

10. *which are used*: see §§ 103 (iv), 109.
11. *in the school*: use при +*prep*.; see § 160.
12. *The food is very good*, обéд (бывáет) óчень вкýсный; *and cheap*: see passage 8, note 13.
13. *the G.C.E. 'O' level examination.* There is no equivalent in Soviet schools; translate Пéрвый госудáрственный экзáмен.
14. *work very hard*: translate 'work very much'.

31   At the Seaside

The Smiths[1] were on holiday in their country cottage in Devon and Robert's school-friend Frank was staying with them. One morning the two boys[2] decided to spend the day at the seaside. They were just about to go,[3] when they heard Michael, Robert's eight-year-old brother, calling them.[4] Dressing as quickly as he could,[5] he announced that he was going with them.

Just after eight o'clock the three of them[6] set off. They walked for several miles along the sandy beach until[7] they found a suitable place for bathing. Here they swam, climbed on the rocks, ate the sandwiches they had brought and sunbathed until[7] it was time[8] to go home. On the way back, however hard he tried,[9] Michael began to fall behind the others. 'If you can't keep up with us, we'll have to leave you on your own.[10] If you get tired so quickly, you should have stayed[11] at home,' Robert called to him. However, they did stop all the same and sat down to wait for him. When Michael caught up with the boys, he asked them coolly:[12] 'Why, what's the matter? Are you that tired?' Robert and Frank laughed and they went on together. It was already quite dark when they reached home. They had ravenous appetites[13] and ate all that Mrs. Smith could find in her larder.

NOTES

For Verbs of Motion, see §§ 127-135; for Indirect Statement and Question, §§ 87-89.

1. *The Smiths*: translate 'Mr Smith with (his) family'.
2. *the two boys*. Two boys, not previously mentioned, два мáльчика; but when already referred to, óба мáльчика, lit. *both boys*.
3. *were just about to go*: see § 126.
4. *they heard Michael . . . calling them*: see §§ 89, 95 (ii).
5. *Dressing*: see § 112; *as quickly as he could*: see § 179.
6. *the three of them*: see § 63.
7. *until*: see § 166.
8. *it was time*: translate 'the time came'.
9. *however hard he tried*: see § 115 (vi).
10. *on your own*: see § 56.
11. *you should have stayed*: see §§ 115 (ii), 189
12. *coolly*: here спокóйно.
13. *ravenous appetites*: use *sing*.

32   The Radio Amateur

Paul had always been good at Physics[1] and had long been interested in radio. He read all the books on the subject[2] that he could find in the School Library and one fine day he said that he had decided to build a wireless set. For six months he saved up all his pocket money, bought all the necessary parts and told his Physics master[3] about his plan. He[4] gave Paul a great deal of advice[5] and even offered to help him build it, but Paul refused his help, as he had firmly resolved to do it on his own.[6]

All through the winter[7] he sat every evening in his room and worked on the set.[8] At last it was ready. He solemnly invited the whole family into his room and asked us all to sit down and listen. Then he switched on the set. At first we could not hear anything. Then there was[9] a deafening crackle. 'Just a moment,' Paul said and turned all the knobs furiously.[10] At last we could hear[11] some music very faintly. Paul turned round and told us proudly that the set was working.[12]

Since then he has made a few improvements and now he can get[13] the B.B.C. quite clearly and sometimes, especially early in the morning, he manages to get[13] foreign stations as well. Now he wants to make a transmitter. Of course this is much more difficult, but I am sure he will do it one day.

NOTES

For the Aspect of Infinitives, see § 100 (ii).

1. *good at Physics*, силён в физике.
2. *on the subject*, в (по) этой области.
3. *Physics master*: see passage 5, note 2.
4. *He*: see passage 6, note 12.
5. *advice*: use *pl.*
6. *on his own*: see § 76.
7. *All through the winter*, в течение всей зимы.
8. *worked on the set*: use над + *instr.*
9. *there was*, послышался.
10. *furiously*: position? see § 16.
11. *At last we could hear*: see § 95 (ii).
12. *that the set was working*: see § 87.
13. *get*: use брать/взять.

33   The Little Dog

When I was a little boy[1] we lived in India, as my father was an officer[2] in the Indian Army. I remember one day my mother, father and I went to the bazaar. We stopped in front of a stall where my mother wanted to buy something. Suddenly a little white dog came running from behind the stall. It was thin[3] and dirty and I felt very sorry for it.[4] The dog ran straight towards[5] a little child that was sitting on the ground. Somebody cried out[6] and everybody ran away,[7] but my father quickly picked up the child and raised it high above his head. The dog turned round[8] and bit my father in the leg.[9] Everybody seemed to be[10] very excited and started[11] looking for a doctor, although my father said it did not hurt very much.[12] The doctor soon appeared. He looked at the wound[13] and then talked to the shopkeeper. Then he looked at Father with a serious expression and said that he would have to be taken to hospital straight away. He added that the dog must be found and destroyed immediately.

Later Mother explained to me that the dog was mad and therefore very dangerous.

NOTES

For Indirect Statement and Question, see §§ 87-89; for rendering the Passive by the Active Voice, see § 109.

1. *When I was a little boy*: see § 27.
2. *was an officer*: see § 31.
3. *thin*: use худой, худенький (*dim.*).
4. *I felt very sorry for it*: see § 137.
5. *towards*: use на + *acc.*
6. *Somebody*: see § 79; *cried out*: see § 95 (i).
7. *everybody ran away*, разбежа́лись (rather than убежа́ли), suggesting 'dispersed', 'scattered'; see also § 159 (ii).

8. *turned round*: see §198.
9. *bit my father in the leg*: see § 48.
10. *seemed to be*: see § 172.
11. *started*, **стáли** (rather than **нáчали**); see §§ 100, 136 (i).
12. *that it did not hurt very much*, **что емý не óчень бóльно**.
13. *He looked at the wound*: see § 187.

34   Moscow

Moscow, the capital of the Soviet Union, was founded by[1] Yury Dolgoruky in 1147, over eight hundred years ago. He built a solitary wooden fortress on the bank of the River Moskva, in the middle of a dense forest. Around it, a city began to grow which was called Moscow.[2] In those far-off days all the houses in the city were wooden.

Nowadays, Moscow is one of the most important and interesting capitals of the world, with a population of almost five million people, excluding the suburbs. It is a city of sharp contrasts. It has[3] magnificent old cathedrals, palaces and countless other historical buildings, beautiful squares, straight, wide avenues and narrow sidestreets with small wooden houses;[4] huge, multistoreyed buildings, comfortable hotels and nine or ten skyscrapers[5] that can be seen[6] from afar. There are over thirty excellent theatres in Moscow, several concert halls and many cinemas. The Bolshoi Theatre is known throughout the world.[7] For many people[8] the new University building[9] on Lenin Hills has become the symbol[10] of the new Moscow. But for most visitors[11] the most beautiful and most remarkable part of the capital is the Kremlin.

NOTES

For Numerals, see §§ 56-60; for Comparatives and Superlatives, §§ 49-55.

1. *was founded by*: see § 109.
2. *which was called Moscow*: see § 175.
3. *It has*: see § 183.
4. *small wooden houses*: see passage 2, note 1.
5. *skyscrapers*. Небоскрёб is only used for the American type; for the Soviet type use высо́тный дом.
6. *can be seen*: see passage 6, note 9.
7. *throughout the world*: translate 'to the whole world'.
8. *For many people*: see § 60 (ii).
9. *the new University building*, но́вое зда́ние МГУ (Моско́вского госуда́рственного университе́та).
10. *has become the symbol*: see § 31.
11. *for most visitors*: see passage 2, note 3.

35 Moscow Transport

Moscow City Transport system serves[1] its citizens well. There are buses, trolley-buses, trams and the underground. There are[2] also many taxis in the streets, and small passenger steamers travel up and down the River Moskva throughout the day.[3]

Muscovites are particularly proud of their Metro.[4] It is[5] one of the most modern underground railways in the world. Some of the stations are very fine, and here you can see interesting examples of Soviet architecture and art. At almost all the stations there are escalators: the passages are clean and light and the trains themselves plain but comfortable. There are no advertisements anywhere, as there are in London. For five copecks[6] you can travel[7] from one end of the city to the other.

The Metro trains and the buses are driven by men,[8] while most of the trams are driven by women.[8] Each bus has[9] two doors, the entrance at the rear and the exit at the front. During the journey[10] both doors are closed and the driver opens them when he stops.[11] The conductress[12] usually sits by the rear door. Many Moscow buses, trolley-buses and trams operate[13] without a conductor. You pay your fare[14] into a box as you enter[15] and tear off a ticket yourself. As in England,[16] the buses, etc. are often overcrowded, especially during rush hour.

NOTES

1. *Transport system*, **систéма трáнспорта**; *serves*: see passage 10, note 2.
2. *There are*: translate 'you can see'; see passage 6, note 9.
3. *throughout the day*, **цéлый день.** For word order of this sentence, see § 15.
4. *their Metro*, **их** or **своё?** see §§ 46, 47.
5. *It is*, **э́то;** see § 74.
6. *For five copecks*: see § 151.
7. *travel*, here **проéхать.**
8. *are driven by men, by women*: see § 109.
9. *Each bus has*: see § 183.
10. *During the journey*, **во врéмя движéния.**
11. *when he stops*, **на останóвке.**
12. *The conductress*: see § 20.
13. *operate*: here **рабóтать.**
14. *your fare*, **за проéзд.**
15. *as you enter*: see § 160.
16. *As in England*, **как у нас (в А́нглии);** see § 158 (iii).

36   A View of Moscow[1]

One day in the spring of 1941 my family and I went to the Sparrow Hills,[2] a range of lovely hills above the Moskva River[3] with a wonderful view of the city. The Sparrow Hills are a favourite place of recreation with Muscovites;[4] I often went there in my youth, but for many years[5] I had had no time for such excursions. It was a clear, sunny day and Moscow lay before us in all her beauty. I suddenly saw how greatly she had changed[6] in those years.[5] On all sides could be seen[7] whole districts of new buildings. Here next to the Kremlin stood the Hotel Moskva, and over there was the new house of the Council of People's Commissars,[8] and the massive building of the Lenin Library.[8] Further off still was the Red Army Theatre,[8] and hundreds of other buildings. Although I had helped to build each one of them, I must say I was struck by the picture as a whole,[9] which was suddenly opened out[10] before me.

This was on the last Sunday in May, 1941. Three weeks later, on just such another Sunday, the war began.[11]   (*Adapted*)

N. CHERNYSHEV: *Moscow, Sketches on the Russian Capital*

NOTES

1. *A View of Moscow*: see § 157 (Note).
2. *Sparrow Hills*, **Воробьёвы го́ры**, now known as **Ле́нинские го́ры**.
3. *above the Moskva River*: translate 'with a view of the Moskva River'; see § 34.
4. *with Muscovites*: translate 'of Muscovites'.
5. *for many years, in those years*: see §§ 163, 164.
6. *I suddenly saw*: see § 95 (ii); *how greatly she had changed*: see § 177.
7. *On all sides*: see passage 2, note 5; *could be seen*, **видне́лись** (see also passage 6, note 9).
8. *the Council of People's Commissars*, **Сове́т Наро́дных Коммисса́ров** (**Совнарко́м**), the former title of the Soviet government (now **Сове́т Мини́стров СССР**); *Lenin Library*, **библиоте́ка и́мени Ле́нина**; *Red Army Theatre*, **теа́тр Кра́сной А́рмии** (now **теа́тр Сове́тской А́рмии**).
9. *I was struck*: see § 109; *by the picture as a whole*, **вся карти́на в це́лом**.
10. *opened out*: see § 103 (iii).
11. *the war began*: see §§ 14, 103 (iii).

37   The Escape

When John joined me at the edge of the river we moved off as fast as we could in a northerly direction.[1] We had[2] only about four more hours of darkness and decided that we must go as far as we could in that time. My maps showed[3] a large wood about ten miles north[4] of the fortress.

Soon after reaching[5] the wood we halted for a few minutes. As we lay[6] on the grass we heard people walking behind us from the direction of[1] the camp. As they passed[6] I recognised two Russians,[7] and one of them was very frightened when I first spoke to them.[8] John and I must have moved[9] very fast, as they had been the first two to escape.[10] We had something to eat together, wished each other the best of luck and then set off again.

By midday the wood was full of Germans, some on bicycles, some on horses. They were whistling and shouting. It was in the evening that what[11] we feared happened. Our group was discovered.[12]

(*University of London, January 1960*)

NOTES

1. *in a northerly direction.* Сторона́ and направле́ние can both mean *direction*; note the use of cases: в каку́ю сто́рону, в како́м направ-ле́нии; *from the direction of,* со стороны́ +gen.
2. *We had*: here нам оста́лось.
3. *My maps showed,* на ка́ртах был обозна́чен.
4. *ten miles*: see § 73; *north,* к се́веру.
5. *Soon after reaching*: see §§ 167-8.
6. *As we lay, as they passed*: see § 173.
7. *two Russians*: see §§ 60 (i), 63.
8. *first,* впервы́е; *spoke to them*: use заговори́ть (*pfv.*).
9. *moved*: use идти́.
10. *had been the first . . . to escape*: translate 'escaped first (пе́рвыми)'.
11. *It was in the evening that*: see § 74; *what*: see § 169.
12. *was discovered*: see § 108.

It was an old grey house, and Dennis passed it every day as he returned from work. He had wondered[1] for a long time whether anyone lived[2] there. One evening he noticed a light on the first floor.[3] Without knowing why, he went up to the front door and rang the bell. There was no reply,[4] but the door was not locked. He opened it himself[5] and entered. There was no light in the hall and he went upstairs. A door opened[6] noiselessly in front of him. There was a woman sitting at a table in the middle of the room, reading a book. She looked at him in silence and then continued reading. As in a dream, Dennis went into the next[7] room. It was quite dark, but he could see[8] a man standing by the window. He seemed to be[9] expecting Dennis. 'Good evening, Mr. Rogers.[10] I am so glad you've come at last. Sit down!' he said in a soft voice.[11] 'You must have forgotten[12] what I told you at[13] our last meeting.' Dennis was certain he had never seen this person before; yet his voice seemed strangely familiar. The stranger continued: 'Before we start talking seriously,[14] I want you to understand[15] that it depends on you, whether[16] our chat is going to be useful and pleasant or not.'

NOTES

For Participles and Gerunds, see §§ 105, 112.

1. *He had wondered*: see § 199.
2. *lived*: tense? see § 88.
3. *on the first floor*: see passage 30, note 7.
4. *There was no reply*: either translate literally or 'they (see § 139) did not reply (or 'open') to him'.
5. *himself*: see § 76.
6. *opened*: see § 103 (iii).
7. *next*: see § 190.
8. *he could see*: see passage 6, note 9.
9. *He seemed to be*: see § 172.

10. *Mr. Rogers.* **Господи́н (госпожа́, *Mrs.*,** *Miss*) is used of foreigners in general; **ми́стер** is sometimes used of Englishmen and Americans; **това́рищ** of Soviet citizens: **Вчера́ ми́стер Макми́ллан и това́рищ Хрущёв встре́тились в Кремле́.**
11. *in a soft voice*: see § 158.
12. *You must have forgotten*: see § 189.
13. *at,* **при** +*prep.*; see § 160.
14. *Before we start talking*: see § 168; *seriously,* **о де́ле.**
15. *I want you to understand*: see § 115 (iii).
16. *whether*: see § 88.

39   The Thaw

It had been an unusually severe winter. The first snow had fállen[1] at the end of October and since then there had been frost[2] and snow-storms almost continuously. The river was frozen and trains had sometimes been days late.[3]

March came and at last there were signs of the end of winter. The temperature rose above zero,[4] it was warmer in the sun and snow began to fall from the roofs. One morning I walked to the centre of the town. It was difficult walking on the wet, slippery snow. I stopped at a street corner wondering where I could have a quick lunch.[5] Here I watched[6] a fat lady crossing[7] the road. In her right hand she was holding a large shopping bag and in her left hand she was carrying a little dog. She kept her balance as best she could[8] during her perilous crossing.[7] When she finally reached the pavement I nodded to her and said: 'Well done!'[9] She looked at me angrily and said: 'How I hate this weather!' But then her expression changed[10] and she added: 'It's poor Fifi I feel sorry for.'[11] I was sorry for[11] the little dog, too, but said nothing this time.[12] 'Never mind,' the lady said, 'I suppose it's a sign of spring,' and continued her unsteady journey[13] along the slippery pavement.

55

NOTES

Special attention should be paid to Word Order (§§ 13-16); for Verbs of Motion, see §§ 127-135; for translation of *to be*, § 122.

1. *The first snow had fallen*: use выпада́ть/вы́пасть.
2. *frost*: use *pl.*
3. *had been days late*: see §§ 63, 151 (iv).
4. *above zero*, вы́ше ноля́; see passage 13, note 5.
5. *where I could have a quick lunch*, где бы на́скоро поза́втракать.
6. *I watched, etc.*: see § 187.
7. *crossing*. The normal words are переходи́ть/перейти́, перехо́д; переправля́ться/перепра́виться, перепра́ва, used of crossing water, would add a humorous effect.
8. *kept her balance*: use баланси́ровать (–и́рую, –и́руешь); *as best she could*, как могла́.
9. *Well done!* Бра́во! Здо́рово! One *can* use молоде́ц of young persons of either sex, when meaning 'well done', 'good chap', but it is inappropriate here.
10. *her expression changed*: see § 177.
11. *I feel sorry for, etc.*: see §§ 137, 143 (Note).
12. *this time*, на э́тот раз.
13. *continued her unsteady journey*: translate 'went on with unsteady steps'; see §§ 24, 134.

40   The Crimea

The Crimea is a large peninsula on the Black Sea. High mountains extend along its southern coast. The climate is subtropical — dry, hot summers[1] and warm, rainy winters[1] — and in the south of the peninsula you can see vineyards and tobacco fields; even oranges and lemons are grown[2] here. The most famous holiday resorts of the Soviet Union are on the Crimean coast — Gurzuf, Yalta, Livadia, a former summer residence of the Russian emperors, and others.

Thousands of Soviet people visit these hospitable towns every year and spend their holidays in comfortable rest homes and sanatoria. The beginnings[3] of the history of the Crimea go back to the days[4] of the ancient Greeks. It is known that Greek merchants traded with the Scythians who lived here, and Tauris (as the Greeks called this region) is mentioned in many Greek legends.

Just over a hundred years[5] ago the Crimea was the scene[6] of a grim[7] and utterly futile war, when Britain, France and Turkey fought for three years against the Russian Empire. Englishmen know 'The Charge of the Light Brigade'[8] by Lord Tennyson; Russians remember that Leo Tolstoy took part in the heroic defence of Sevastopol.

Fierce fighting also took place[9] in the Crimea during the Second World War. In 1945 an historic conference was held at Yalta between Churchill, Roosevelt and Stalin,[10] at which[11] plans for the final defeat and the division of Germany were worked out.[12]

NOTES

Particular attention should be paid to Word Order; see §§ 13-16.

1. *summers, winters*: use *sing.*
2. *are grown*: see §§103 (iv), 109.
3. *The beginnings*: use *sing.*
4. *go back to*: use относи́ться к + *dat.*; *the days*: translate 'the times'.
5. *Just over a hundred years*, сто лет с ли́шним.
6. *the scene*: use теа́тр.
7. *grim*: use жесто́кий, *cruel.*
8. *The Charge of the Light Brigade*, «Налёт Ула́нской брига́ды».
9. *Fierce fighting took place*, шли ожесточённые бои́.
10. *Churchill*, Че́рчилль; *Roosevelt*, Ру́звельт, see § 201; *Stalin*, Ста́лин (*instr.* Ста́линым).
11. *at which*, во вре́мя кото́рой.
12. *were worked out*: see §§103 (iv), 108.

UNANNOTATED 'O' LEVEL EXAMINATION PASSAGES

I

'Do you want to come with me?' she asked, putting on her coat and walking towards the door. 'If you don't come now it will be too late. In any case they'll be waiting for me at the corner.' I said nothing, but walked towards the window and looked out at the rain falling on the dark street. She thought I was afraid, I suppose. She stood at the door with her hands in the pockets of her overcoat. 'Well, are you coming or aren't you?'

I lit a cigarette and continued to look out of the window. It's silly, I thought. If I tell her the truth, she'll never leave this house — with or without me. And yet she *must* go. How can I make her understand? If only she would realize that I could help her more by staying behind. 'All right,' I said. 'I am afraid. You'd better go alone.'

(*University of Cambridge Local Examinations Syndicate, July 1958*)

II

My parents sometimes go abroad, and last year they said I should go with them. Usually I spend the holidays with an old aunt, so I was pleased to go. We went by steamer to France and stayed in a small town on the coast. There were not many English people there and I had to speak French quite a lot. I was able to understand what I heard, but I found it difficult to speak myself. The town was very similar to all such places; the houses were taller than in England and there were fewer cars in the streets. The hotel where we lived was very comfortable and I liked my room, which had a large window. For breakfast we ate bread and butter and we drank coffee. After breakfast we went each day to the sea — I bathed and my mother and father sat in the sun. My mother read a novel and my father

slept. All this we could have done at the seaside in England, and I do not understand why we went to France at all. Next time I hope to go to Paris, which is much more interesting. (*Adapted*)
(*Oxford and Cambridge Schools Examination Board, December 1958*)

III

Dear Ivan,

I have been very busy the last two or three months, so please forgive me for not answering your letter sooner. I have had to prepare for my examinations. Now they're over and I'm waiting for the results. I worked very hard. I even stopped playing tennis and swimming, although it was a beautiful summer. We've had weeks and weeks of warm, sunny weather, and it was hard having to stay indoors and sit at a desk covered with books.

Now that the exams are over I am writing a few letters, which I should have written long ago. I've had some short holidays — once I went up the Thames by boat to Oxford, another time I went by bus to Stratford, where I visited Shakespeare's birth-place. I have also walked a lot in Scotland. In your last letter you didn't tell me what you were going to do during your holidays in the summer. Do write and let me know.

Yours,
John
(*University of London, Summer 1960*)

IV

After he had stood there for about five minutes I decided that it was time I said something. I noticed that he had not lit the cigarette which I had given him. I asked him: 'Don't you want to smoke?' As soon as he heard my voice he turned round from the window and looked at me steadily for a moment. Then he walked over to the table, picked up a box of matches and lit his cigarette.

He sat down in the armchair at the other end of the room. 'I have been wanting to talk to you for a long time,' he said at last. 'But I had to wait for a suitable opportunity. Now that your wife has left town you will be prepared to hear what I have to say. Sit down over there' — he pointed to the sofa — 'and listen to me very carefully.'

(*University of Cambridge Local Examinations Syndicate, July 1960*)

V

My father works in London and goes to work by train. He always comes home at exactly seven o'clock. One evening recently it was already half-past seven and he had not arrived. It was dark and wet, and my mother began to worry. 'Perhaps he is still busy at the office?' — I suggested. 'No,' she replied, 'he always tells me, if he has to work late. He said nothing about it this morning. Please go to the station and find out if the train is late.' I went to the station — it is quite near our house — and asked if the train had arrived. 'Yes,' said the man, 'ten minutes ago.' I went home again. My mother rang the office — he was not there, and she was sure that something had happened to him. I did not know what to do. Suddenly we heard someone open the door. Father came into the room. We stood up and mother cried: 'Where have you been? How did you come from London?' My father smiled and said: 'I came in our car. I have just bought it.'

(*Oxford and Cambridge Schools Examination Board, December 1960*)

Vocabulary

able, to be, мочь (могу́, мо́жешь... мо́гут; мог, –ла́, –ло́)/с–; **one can**, мо́жно; **cannot**, нельзя́, невозмо́жно
about (concerning), о (об, о́бо) + *prep*.; (around) о́коло +*gen*.; **be — to**, собира́ться + *infin*.
above, над +*instr*.
abroad, за грани́цей; (*mtn*.) за грани́цу; **from —**, из-за грани́цы
accent, акце́нт
across, че́рез, сквозь +*acc*.; *adv*. поперёк
action, де́йствие
actor, актёр
add, прибавля́ть/приба́вить (приба́влю, приба́вишь)
address, а́дрес, *pl*. –а́, –о́в
advertisement, объявле́ние
advice, сове́т
adviser, сове́тник
aeroplane, самолёт
afraid, to be, боя́ться (бою́сь, бои́шься)/по– +*gen*.
after, по́сле +*gen*.; че́рез +*acc*.; *conj*. по́сле того́, как; **— all**, всё-таки́
afterwards, пото́м, зате́м
again, опя́ть, сно́ва; ещё раз
ago, тому́ наза́д; давно́; **not long —**, неда́вно
agree, быть согла́сным; **I —**, я согла́сен, –сна
air, во́здух
airport, аэропо́рт
Alexeyevka, Алексе́евка
all, весь (вся, всё, все); **— right**, хорошо́; **— the same**, всё-таки́
allowed, to be, мо́жно + *dat*.; **not —**, нельзя́ + *dat*.
almost, почти́
alone, оди́н, одна́, одно́
along, по + *dat*.; вдоль +*gen*.
aloud, вслух
also, то́же, та́кже; и; ещё
although, хотя́

always, всегда́
amusing, заба́вный, *sht.fm.* –вен, –вна, –вно
ancient, стари́нный; дре́вний, –яя, –ее
and, и, а; **— so**, так что, и поэ́тому
angry, серди́тый, *sht.fm.* серди́т, –а, –о
animal, живо́тное
announce, объявля́ть/объяви́ть (объявлю́, объя́вишь)
another, друго́й; про́чий; ещё
answer, отве́т; *vb*. отвеча́ть/отве́тить (отве́чу, отве́тишь)
anxious, озабо́ченный, *sht.fm.* –чен, –чена
any, како́й-нибудь; **in — case**, во вся́ком слу́чае; **not — more**, бо́льше не
anybody, anyone, кто́-нибудь; **not —**, никто́
anyway, во вся́ком слу́чае
appear, появля́ться, появи́ться (появлю́сь, поя́вишься)
appetite, аппети́т; **ravenous —**, во́лчий (–чья, –чье) аппети́т
apple, я́блоко, *pl*. я́блоки, я́блок
Aral Sea, Ара́льское мо́ре
architecture, архитекту́ра
armchair, кре́сло, *pl*. –сла, –сел
army, а́рмия
around, вокру́г +*gen*.
arrival, прихо́д; прие́зд
arrive, приходи́ть (–хожу́, –хо́дишь)/прийти́ (–ду́, –дёшь; –шёл, –шла́); приезжа́ть/прие́хать (–е́ду, –е́дешь)
art, иску́сство
artist, худо́жник
as, как; (when) когда́; (since) так как; **— far — we could**, как мо́жно да́льше; **— well**, то́же, та́кже, и; **— soon —**, как то́лько
Asia, А́зия; **Central —**, Центра́льная А́зия

ask, спра́шивать/спроси́ть (спрошу́, спро́сишь); — **for**, проси́ть (прошу́, про́сишь)/по- + *gen.*
at, в, на + *prep.*; в + *acc.*; у + *gen.*; при + *prep.*; за + *instr.*; — **once**, сра́зу (же), сейча́с (же), то́тчас (же)
attendant, проводни́к; *f.* проводни́ца
attentive, внима́тельный, *sht.fm.* –лен, –льна, –льно
aunt, тётя
Austria, А́встрия
autumn, о́сень *f.*; **in —**, о́сенью
avenue, проспе́кт
await, ожида́ть, no *pfv.*; ждать (жду, ждёшь)/подо- + *acc.* or *gen.*

baker, бу́лочник
bank, бе́рег (на берегу́), *pl.* –а́, –ов
bare, го́лый, *sht.fm.* гол, –а́, –о
barely, едва́ (ли)
barn, амба́р; сара́й
basket, корзи́на, корзи́нка
bathe, купа́ться/вы́–
bathing, купа́ние; — **costume**, купа́льный костю́м
bathroom, ва́нная
bazaar, база́р
B.B.C., Би-Би-Си
be, быть (*pres.* есть; *past* был, –ла́, –ло; *fut.* бу́ду, бу́дешь); — (**supposed) to**, see *due*
beach, пляж
bear, медве́дь *m.*
beauty, красота́
because, потому́ что; — **of**, из-за + *gen.*
become, станови́ться (становлю́сь, стано́вишься)/стать (ста́ну, ста́нешь); де́латься/с–; all + *instr.*
bed, посте́ль *f.*; крова́ть *f.*; **go to —**, ложи́ться/лечь (ля́гу, ля́жешь; лёг, легла́) спать; идти́ (иду́, идёшь; шёл, шла)/по– спать
bedroom, спа́льня, *g.pl.* –лен
before, до + *gen.*; пе́ред + *instr.*; *conj.* до того́, как; пе́ред тем, как; пре́жде чем; *adv.* пре́жде, ра́ньше
begin, начина́ть/нача́ть (начну́, начнёшь); начина́ться/нача́ться

62

beginning, нача́ло
behave, вести́ (веду́, ведёшь; вёл, вела́) себя́
behind, за + *instr.*; позади́ + *gen.*
bell, звоно́к, звонка́; **church** — etc., ко́локол, *pl.* –а́, –о́в
belong, принадлежа́ть (–лежу́, –лежи́шь) + *dat.*, no *pfv.*
bench, скамья́; *dim.* скаме́йка, *g.pl.* –е́ек
beneath, под + *instr.*
Berlin, Берли́н
besides, кро́ме того́
between, ме́жду + *instr.*
bicycle, весолипе́д
big, большо́й, –а́я, –о́е, *sht.fm.* вели́к, –а́, –о
bird, пти́ца; *dim.* пти́чка, *g.pl.* –чек
birth-place, ме́сто рожде́ния, ро́дина
bite, куса́ть/укуси́ть (укушу́, уку́сишь)
black, чёрный
blanket, одея́ло
blood, кровь *f.*
bloom, цвет; **in full —**, в по́лном цвету́
blow, дуть (ду́ю, ду́ешь)/по–
blue, голубо́й; си́ний, –яя, –ее
boat, ло́дка, *g.pl.* –док
bold, сме́лый, *sht.fm.* смел, –а́, –о
book, кни́га; *dim.* кни́жка, *g.pl.*–жек
bookcase, кни́жный шкаф; эта-же́рка, *g.pl.* –рок
boot, боти́нок, боти́нка
bored, to be, мне ску́чно; **I got —**, мне ста́ло ску́чно
boss, хозя́ин, *pl.* хозя́ева, хозя́ев
both, о́ба (*f.* о́бе)
bottle, буты́лка, *g.pl.* –лок
bottom, дно
box, я́щик; **match —**, коро́бка (*g.pl.* –бок) спи́чек
boy, ма́льчик
bread, хлеб
breakfast, за́втрак; **to have —**, за́втракать/по–
breathe, дыша́ть (дышу́, ды́шишь) + *instr.*
breeze, ветеро́к, ветерка́
Brest, Брест
bright, я́ркий, *sht.fm.* я́рок, ярка́, я́рко
brilliant, блестя́щий, –ая, –ее

bring, приноси́ть (–ношу́, –но́-
сишь)/принести́ (–несу́, –несёшь; –нёс, –несла́); при-
води́ть (–вожу́, –во́дишь)/при-
вести́ (–веду́, –ведёшь; –вёл,
–вела́); привози́ть (–вожу́,
–во́зишь)/привезти́ (–везу́,
–везёшь; –вёз, –везла́)

Britain, А́нглия, Великобрита́ния

broad, широ́кий, *sht.fm.* широ́к,
–а́, –о́

brother, брат, *pl.* –ья, –ьев

build, стро́ить/по-

building, зда́ние; постро́йка, *g.pl.*
–о́ек

bun, бу́лка, *g.pl.* –лок

bundle, у́зел, узла́

bunk, ко́йка, *g.pl.* ко́ек

burn, горе́ть (горю́, гори́шь)/за–;
burning, горя́щий, –ая, –ее

bus, авто́бус; **— stop,** остано́вка
авто́буса

business, де́ло, *pl.* дела́, дел

busy, за́нятый, *sht.fm.* за́нят, –а́, –о

but, но, а

butcher, мясни́к

butter, ма́сло

buy, покупа́ть/купи́ть (куплю́,
ку́пишь)

cabbage, капу́ста, no *pl.*

calf, телёнок, телёнка, *pl.* теля́та,
теля́т

call, звать (зову́, зовёшь)/по–; на-
зыва́ть/назва́ть; **to be —ed,**
называ́ться/назва́ться; **— on**
(visit), заходи́ть (–хожу́, –хо́-
дишь)/зайти́ (–йду́, –йдёшь;
–шёл, –шла́) к + *dat.*; **— out,** кри-
ча́ть (кричу́, кричи́шь)/по–, за–,
кри́кнуть (кри́кну, кри́кнешь)

camp, ла́герь, *m.pl.* –я́, –е́й

can, cannot, see **able, to be**

canteen, столо́вая

capital, столи́ца

car, автомоби́ль *m.*, маши́на

careful, (cautious) осторо́жный,
sht.fm. –жен, –жна, –жно; (attentive) внима́тельный, *sht.fm.*
–лен, –льна, –льно

carriage, ваго́н

carrots, морко́вь, *f.*, no *pl.*

carry, носи́ть (ношу́, но́сишь)–
нести́ (несу́, несёшь; нёс, не-

сла́)/понести́; вози́ть (вожу́,
во́зишь)–везти́ (везу́, везёшь;
вёз, везла́)/повезти́

case, слу́чай; **in any —,** во
вся́ком слу́чае; и без того́

castle, за́мок, за́мка

catch, лови́ть (ловлю́, ло́вишь)/
пойма́ть; **— up with,** догоня́ть/
догна́ть (–гоню́, –го́нишь)

cathedral, собо́р

centre, центр, среди́на

certain, уве́ренный, *sht.fm.* уве́рен,
–а, –ы

chain, цепь *f.*; *dim.* цепо́чка, *g.pl.*
–чек

chair, стул, *pl.* –лья, –льев

change, меня́ть(ся), переменя́ть-
(ся)/–и́ть(ся), изменя́ть(ся)/
–и́ть(ся); (clothes) переодева́ть-
ся/переоде́ться (–де́нусь, –де́-
нешься); (trains) переса́живать-
ся/пересе́сть (–ся́ду, –ся́дешь;
–сел, –а), де́лать/с– переса́дку

chat, бесе́да; *vb.* бесе́довать (бесе́-
дую, бесе́дуешь)/по–

cheap, дешёвый, *sht.fm.* дёшев,
дешева́, дёшево

cheerful, весёлый, *sht.fm.* ве́сел,
–а́, –о

cheese, сыр, *part.gen.* сы́ру

chemistry, хи́мия; *adj.* хими́ческий

chest-of-drawers, комо́д

child, ребёнок, ребёнка, *pl.* де́ти,
–е́й (ребя́та, ребя́т)

childhood, де́тство

choice, вы́бор

choose, выбира́ть/вы́брать (–беру,
–берёшь)

Christmas, Рождество́

church, це́рковь *f.*, це́ркви, *instr.*
це́рковью

cigarette, папиро́са

cinema, кино́ *indecl.*, кинотеа́тр

citizen, граждани́н, *pl.* гра́ждане,
гра́ждан; жи́тель *m.* (го́рода)

city, го́род, *pl.* –а́, –о́в; *adj.* город-
ско́й

civil, гражда́нский

class, класс; **—room,** кла́ссная
ко́мната

clean, чи́стый, *sht.fm.* чист, –а́, –о

clear, я́сный, *sht.fm.* я́сен, ясна́,
я́сно; (distinct) отчётливый,
sht.fm. –ив, –а, –о

climate, кли́мат
climb, ла́зить (ла́жу, ла́зишь)
  –лезть (ле́зу, ле́зешь; лез,
  ле́зла)/поле́зть; — **down**,
  слеза́ть/слезть
close (stuffy), ду́шный, *sht.fm.*
  –шен, –шна́, –шно
close (near), бли́зко от + *gen.*
close, закрыва́ть/закры́ть (–кро́ю,
  –кро́ешь), *p.p.p.* закры́тый
clothes, оде́жда, no *pl.*
coast, бе́рег (на берегу́), *pl.* –а́, –о́в
coat, пальто́ *indecl.*
coffee, ко́фе *m.*, *indecl.*
cold, просту́да; *adj.* холо́дный,
  sht.fm. хо́лоден, холодна́, –о
colour, цвет, *pl.* –а́, –о́в; кра́ска,
  g.pl. –сок
come, ходи́ть (хожу́, хо́дишь)–
  идти́ (иду́, идёшь; шёл, шла);
  приходи́ть/прийти́; е́здить
  (е́зжу, е́здишь)– е́хать (е́ду,
  е́дешь); приезжа́ть/прие́хать;
  (seasons, etc.) наступа́ть/–и́ть;
  — **and see**, заходи́ть/зайти́,
  заезжа́ть/зае́хать к + *dat.*;
  — **back**, возвраща́ться/верну́ть-
  ся; — **close**, приближа́ться/
  –бли́зиться (–жусь, –зишься)
  к + *dat.*; — **down**, сходи́ть/сойти́;
  — **into**, входи́ть/войти́, въез-
  жа́ть/въе́хать в + *acc.*; — **up to**,
  подходи́ть/подойти́ к + *dat.*
comfortable, удо́бный, *sht.fm.* –бен,
  –бна, –бна
compare, сра́внивать/сравни́ть
compartment, купе́ *indecl.*
completely, вполне́, соверше́нно
composer, компози́тор
concert, конце́рт; — **hall**, конце́рт-
  ный зал
conductor, конду́ктор, *pl.* –а́, –о́в
conductress, конду́ктор, конду́к-
  торша
conference, конфере́нция
conquer, завоёвывать/завоева́ть
  (завою́ю, завою́ешь)
consist, состоя́ть (–стою́, –стои́шь)
  из + *gen.*
continue, продолжа́ть(ся)/
  –и́ть(ся)
continuous, продолжи́тельный,
  sht.fm. –лен, –льна, –льно;
  сплошно́й

64

contrary, on the, напро́тив
contrast, контра́ст
conversation, разгово́р, бесе́да
cooking, use стол or пи́ща
cool, прохла́дный, *sht.fm.* –ден,
  –дна, –дно
copeck, копе́йка, *g.pl.* –е́ек
copse, ро́ща, *dim.* ро́щица
copy out, перепи́сывать/пере-
  писа́ть (–пишу́, –пи́шешь)
corner, у́гол, угла́ (на углу́)
correspond, перепи́сываться с +
  instr.
cost, сто́ить
cosy, ую́тный, *sht.fm.* –тен, –тна,
  –тно
cough, ка́шель, ка́шля; *vb.* ка́ш-
  лять/ка́шлянуть
count, счита́ть/сосчита́ть
counter, прила́вок, прила́вка
countless, бесчи́сленный, *sht.fm.*
  –лен, –ленна, –ленно
country, страна́; — **side**, дере́вня;
  in the —, в дере́вне, за́ городом; — **cottage**, да́ча (на да́че)
course, of, коне́чно, разуме́ется
cover, покрыва́ть/покры́ть (–кро́ю,
  –кро́ешь); *p.p.p.* покры́тый
cow, коро́ва; — **shed**, коро́вник,
  хлев
crackle, треск
cramped, те́сный, *sht.fm.* –сен,
  –сна́, –сно
cricket, кри́кет
Crimea, Крым (в Крыму́); **Crimean**, кры́мский
cross, серди́тый, *sht.fm.* серди́т,
  –а, –о
cross (*vb.*), переходи́ть/перейти́
  (–йду́, –йдёшь; –шёл, –шла́)
  че́рез + *acc.*
crowd, толпа́, мно́го наро́ду
crowded, we are, нам те́сно
cry, крича́ть (кричу́, кричи́шь)/
  по–, за–, кри́кнуть (кри́кну,
  кри́кнешь)
customer, покупа́тель *m.*, клие́нт

damp, сыро́й, *sht.fm.* сыр, –а́, –о
dangerous, опа́сный, *sht.fm.* –сен,
  –сна, –сно
dark, тёмный, *sht.fm.* тёмен, –мна́,
  –мно́; *n.* темнота́

darkness, темнота
daughter, дочь, дочери; *dim.* дочка,
g.pl. дочек
day, день, дня; (twenty-four hours)
сутки, суток, *pl.* only; one —,
однажды; когда-то (-нибудь)
deafening, оглушительный, *sht.fm.*
–лен, –льна, –льно
deal, a great deal of, see *much*
dear, дорогой, *sht.fm.* дорог, –а,
–о; *comp.* дороже
December, декабрь *m.*
decide, решать/–йть
defeat, поражение; разгром
defence, оборона
dense, густой, *sht.fm.* густ, –а, –о
department store, универсальный
магазин (универмаг)
depend, зависеть (–вишу, –висишь)
от + *gen.*
desert, пустыня
deserted, пустынный, *sht.fm.* –нен,
–нна, –нно
desk, письменный стол
destroy, истреблять/истребить
(–треблю, –требишь), уничто-
жать/-ить
dialogue, диалог
dictation, диктант, диктовка
different, разный
difficult, трудный, *sht.fm.* –ден,
–дна, –дно
dining-car, вагон-ресторан
dining-room, столовая
dinner, обед; have —, обедать/по–
direction, направление (в этом на-
правлении); сторона (в эту сто-
рону
dirty, грязный, *sht.fm.* –зен, –зна,
–зно
disappear, исчезать/исчезнуть
(–чезну, –чезнешь; –чез, –чезла)
discover, обнаруживать/обнару-
жить; *p.p.p.* обнаруженный
distance, расстояние; from a —,
издалека
district, район, квартал (города)
division, деление
do, делать/с–
doctor, доктор, *pl.* –а, –ов; врач
dog, собака; *dim.* собачка, *g.pl.*
–чек
door, дверь *f.*; front —, парадная
дверь

down, вниз
downstairs, внизу; *mtn.* вниз
drawer, ящик
dream, сон, сна; мечта; *vb.* видеть
во сне; мечтать
dreary, унылый, *sht.fm.* уныл, –а,
–о
dress, платье, *pl.* –ья, –ьев; *vb.* оде-
вать/одеть (одену, оденешь);
одеваться/одеться
drink, пить (пью, пьёшь)/вы–
drive, ездить (езжу, ездишь)–ехать
(еду, едешь)/поехать; — a car,
водить (вожу, водишь)–вести
(веду, ведёшь; вёл, вела) ма-
шину; управлять, править
(правлю, правишь) машиной
driver, шофёр, водитель
dry, сухой, *sht.fm.* сух, –а, –о;
comp. суше
due, to be, должен, –жна, –жно
dull, скучный, *sht.fm.* –чен, –чна,
–чно
during, во время + *gen.*
dusk, сумерки, сумерек, *pl.* only
dust, пыль *f.*
dusty, пыльный, *sht.fm.* пылен,
–льна, –льно

each, каждый; — **other**, друг друга,
друг от друга, друг с другом,
etc.
early, ранний, –яя, –ее; *adv.* рано;
comp. раньше
earth, земля, *instr.* землёй
easy, лёгкий, *sht.fm.* лёгок, –гка,
–гко; *comp.* легче
eat, есть (ем, ешь, ест, едим,
едите, едят; ел, –а, –о)/съ–, по–;
кушать/с–, по–
edge, край (на краю), *pl.* –я, –ёв
egg, яйцо, *pl.* яйца, яйц
Egypt, Египет
eight, восемь; **eight hundred**, во-
семьсот; **eight-year-old**, восьми-
летний, –яя, –ее
either . . . or, или . . . или; **not . . .
either**, тоже не
elderly, пожилой, (уже) не молодой
eleven, одиннадцать; **eleven hundred and forty-seven**, тысяча сто
сорок семь (седьмой)

65

emperor, импера́тор
empire, импе́рия; **Russian** —, Росси́йская Импе́рия
empty, пусто́й, *sht.fm.* пуст, –а́, –о
end, коне́ц, конца́; **in the** —, наконе́ц, в конце́ концо́в
endless, бесконе́чный, *sht.fm.* –чен, –чна, –чно
engine, мото́р
engineer, инжене́р
England, А́нглия
English, англи́йский
Englishman, англича́нин, *pl.* англича́не, англича́н
enjoy, наслажда́ться/наслади́ться (–слажу́сь, –слади́шься) + *instr.*; (like) use нра́виться (нра́влюсь, нра́вишься)/по– + *dat.*
enjoyable, прия́тный, *sht.fm.* –тен, –тна, –тно
enough, доста́точно + *gen.*; дово́льно
enter, входи́ть (–хожу́, –хо́дишь)/войти́ (–йду́, –йдёшь; –шёл, –шла) в + *acc.*; въезжа́ть/въе́хать (–е́ду, –е́дешь) в + *acc.*
entirely, по́лностью, исключи́тельно
entrance, вход; въезд
envelope, конве́рт
escalator, эскала́тор
escape, побе́г, бе́гство; *vb.* бежа́ть (бегу́, бежи́шь . . . бегу́т)
especially, осо́бенно
etc., и так да́лее (и т. д.)
Europe, Евро́па
even, да́же, и
evening, ве́чер, *pl.* –а́, –о́в; **in the** —, ве́чером
every, ка́ждый
everybody, everyone, все *pl.*; —**thing,** всё; —**where,** везде́, всю́ду
exactly, то́чно; (of time) ро́вно
examination, экза́мен
example, приме́р; образе́ц, образца́; **for** —, наприме́р
excellent, превосхо́дный, *sht.fm.* –ден, –дна, –дно
except, кро́ме, за исключе́нием + *gen.*
excited, to be, волнова́ться (волну́юсь, волну́ешься)/вз–
exclaim, восклица́ть/воскли́кнуть (–кли́кну, –кли́кнешь)

excluding, не счита́я + *gen.*
excursion, экску́рсия; прогу́лка, *g.pl.* –лок
excuse, извиня́ть/–и́ть
exit, вы́ход
expect, ожида́ть + *acc.* or *gen.*
expensive, дорого́й, *sht.fm.* до́рог, –а́, –о; *comp.* доро́же
explain, объясня́ть/–и́ть
expression, выраже́ние
extend, простира́ться, тяну́ться (тяну́сь, тя́нешься)
eye, глаз, *pl.* глаза́, глаз

face, лицо́, *pl.* ли́ца, лиц
fact, факт; **in** —, действи́тельно, в са́мом де́ле
factory, заво́д (на заво́де)
faint, сла́бый, *sht.fm.* слаб, –а́, –о
fairy tale, ска́зка, *g.pl.* –зок
fall, па́дать/упа́сть (упаду́, упадёшь; упа́л, упа́ла); — **asleep,** засыпа́ть/засну́ть (–сну́, –снёшь); — **behind,** отстава́ть (–стаю́, –стаёшь)/отста́ть (–ста́ну, –ста́нешь) от + *gen.*
familiar, знако́мый, *sht.fm.* знако́м, –а, –о
family, семья́; **as a** —, всей семьёй
famous, знамени́тый, *sht.fm.* знамени́т, –а, –о
far, far away, далеко́; **far off** (*adj.*), давно́ мину́вший, отдалённый
farm, фе́рма
farmer, фе́рмер
fast, бы́стрый, *sht.fm.* быстр, –а́, –о; ско́рый, *sht.fm.* скор, –а́, –о
fat, то́лстый, *sht.fm.* толст, –а́, –о
father, оте́ц, отца́; па́па
favourite, люби́мый
fear, боя́ться (бою́сь, бои́шься)/по– + *gen.*
February, февра́ль *m.*
feed, корми́ть (кормлю́, ко́рмишь)/по–
feel, чу́вствовать (чу́вствую, чу́вствуешь)/по– (себя́); **I — like** (want) мне хо́чется
fellow passenger, спу́тник; *fem.* спу́тница
few, немно́го, не́сколько, ма́ло + *gen.*; немно́гие; —**er,** ме́ньше
field, по́ле, *pl.* –я́, –е́й
fifth, пя́тый

fight, дра́ться (деру́сь, дерёшься)/
по–; воева́ть (вою́ю, вою́ешь)
с + *instr.*

figure, фигу́ра; *dim.* фигу́рка

film, фильм, кинофи́льм

final, оконча́тельный; **finally**, на-
коне́ц, в конце́ концо́в

find, находи́ть (–хожу́, –хо́дишь)/
найти́ (–йду́, –йдёшь; –шёл,
–шла́); — **out**, узнава́ть (узнаю́,
узнаёшь)/узна́ть

fine, прекра́сный, *sht.fm.* –сен,
–сна, –сно

fire, ого́нь, огня́; —**place**, ками́н

firm, твёрдый, *sht.fm.* твёрд, –а́, –о

first, пе́рвый; **at** —, снача́ла,
сперва́

five, пять; **five hundred**, пятьсо́т

flat, кварти́ра

floor, пол (на полу́); (storey) эта́ж,
g.pl. –же́й

flower, цвето́к, цветка́, *pl.* цветы́,
–о́в

fly, лета́ть–лете́ть (лечу́, лети́шь)/
полете́ть; — **away**, улета́ть/
улете́ть

fog, тума́н; **foggy**, тума́нный, *sht.*
fm. –нен, –нна, –нно

follow (understand), следи́ть (сле-
жу́, следи́шь) за + *instr.*

fond, to be — **of**, люби́ть (люблю́,
лю́бишь)/по–

food, пи́ща, еда́

foot, нога́; **on** —, пешко́м

football, футбо́л

for, для + *gen.*; за + *acc.*, + *instr.*;
на + *acc.*; по + *dat.*; от + *gen.*;
conj. так как

foreign, ниостра́нный, зарубе́ж-
ный

foreigner, иностра́нец, иностра́нца,
pl. –нцы, –нцев

forest, лес (в лесу́), *pl.* –а́, –о́в

forget, забыва́ть/забы́ть (–бу́ду,
–бу́дешь)

forgive, проща́ть/прости́ть (про-
щу́, прости́шь)

form, класс; — **eight**, восьмо́й
класс

former, бы́вший

fortress, кре́пость *f.*

found, осно́вывать/основа́ть

four ую́, –уёшь)
(–, че́тыре; **fourteen**, четы́рнад-
цать; **fourteen-year-old**, четыр-
надцатиле́тний, –яя, –ее

fox, лиса́, лиси́ца

France, Фра́нция (во Фра́нции)

freeze, замерза́ть/замёрзнуть
(–зну, –знешь; –мёрз, –мёрзла)

French, францу́зский

frequently, ча́сто

fresh, све́жий, *sht.fm.* свеж, –а́, –о́

Friday, пя́тница

friend, друг, *pl.* друзья́, друзе́й

friendly, приве́тливый, *sht.fm.* при-
ве́тлив, –а, –о

frightened, испу́ганный, *sht.fm.*
–ган, –а, –о; **be** —, пуга́ться/ис–

frock, пла́тье, *pl.* –ья, –ьев

from, от + *gen.*; из + *gen.*; с + *gen.*;
у + *gen.*; по + *dat.*; — **behind**,
из-за + *gen.*

front (*adj.*), пере́дний, –яя, –ее; **in**
— **of**, пе́ред + *instr.*; **at the** —,
впереди́, спе́реди

frontier, грани́ца, *instr.* грани́цей

frost, моро́з

frown, хму́риться/на–

fruit, фру́кты, фру́ктов

full, по́лный, *sht.fm.* –лон, –лна́,
–лно́ + *gen.*

furiously, бе́шено

further, further away, да́льше от
+ *gen.*

futile, бессмы́сленный, *sht.fm.*
–лен, –ленна, –ленно

game, игра́; **games**, спорти́вные
и́гры

garden, сад (в саду́); *dim.* са́дик

gate, воро́та, –о́т, *pl.* only; (small)
кали́тка, *gen.pl.* –ток

general, генера́л; полково́дец,
полково́дца

Geneva, Жене́ва

gentle, мя́гкий, *sht.fm.* мя́гок, –гка́,
–ко; лёгкий, *sht.fm.* лёгок, –гка́,
–гко .

German, не́мец, не́мца, *pl.* –мцы,
–мцев; *adj.* неме́цкий

Germany, Герма́ния

get, достава́ть (–стаю́, –стаёшь)/
доста́ть (–ста́ну, –ста́нешь); —
off, выходи́ть (–хожу́, –хо́дишь)/
вы́йти (–йду, –йдешь, –шел,
–шла) из + *gen.*; сходи́ть/сойти́
с + *gen.*: — **on**, сади́ться (сажу́сь,

сади́шься)/сесть (ся́ду, ся́дешь;
сел, –а) в + acc.; — out, выни-
ма́ть/вы́нуть (–ну, –нешь) из +
gen.; (alight from), see get off;
— tired, устава́ть (устаю́, уста-
ёшь)/уста́ть (уста́ну, уста́нешь);
— to, попада́ть/попа́сть (–паду́,
–падёшь; –па́л, –па́ла) в, на +
acc., к + dat.; — up, встава́ть
(встаю́, встаёшь)/встать (вста́-
ну, вста́нешь); — used to, при-
выка́ть/привы́кнуть (past при-
вы́к, –ла) к + dat.
girl, де́вочка, g.pl. –чек; де́вушка,
g.pl. –шек
give, дава́ть (даю́, даёшь)/дать
(дам, дашь, даст, дади́м,
дади́те, даду́т) + dat.
glad, рад, –а, –ы
glass, стекло́; drinking —, стака́н;
glasses (spectacles), очки́, очко́в
go, ходи́ть (хожу́, хо́дишь)–идти́
(иду́, идёшь; шёл, шла)/пойти́;
е́здить (е́зжу, е́здишь)–е́хать
(е́ду, е́дешь)/пое́хать; — away,
уходи́ть/уйти́; уезжа́ть/уе́хать;
— back, возвраща́ться/верну́ть-
ся (верну́сь, вернёшься); — by,
проходи́ть/пройти́ (ми́мо); —
into, входи́ть/войти́ в + acc.; —
off, уходи́ть/уйти́, пойти́ (pfv.);
— on (continue), продолжа́ть-
(ся)/–ить(ся); — out, выходи́ть/
вы́йти из + gen.; — boating, skating, skiing, sledging, ката́ться/
по– на ло́дке, на конька́х, на
лы́жах, на саня́х/сала́зках; —ing
to, use собира́ться or fut.
gold (adj.), золото́й
good, хоро́ший, –ая, –ее, sht.fm.
хоро́ш, –а́, –о́; comp. лу́чше,
лу́чший; sup. (са́мый) лу́чший;
(kind) до́брый, sht.fm. добр, –а́,
–о
good-bye, до свида́ния; say —,
проща́ться/по– с + instr.
goodness, my, Бо́же мой!
goods, това́ры, това́ров
Gorky Library, библиоте́ка и́мени
Го́рького
grammar, грамма́тика
grandfather, дед, де́душка; grandmother, ба́бушка; grandparents,
де́душка с ба́бушкой

grass, трава́
great, вели́кий, sht.fm. вели́к, –а́
–о; a — deal, о́чень мно́го;
greatly, си́льно
Greek, грек; adj. гре́ческий
green, зелёный
greet, приве́тствовать (–ую,
–уешь); здоро́ваться/по– с +
instr.
grey, се́рый; grey-haired, седо́й
groceries, прови́зия, бакале́я (no
pl.)
grocer's shop, продово́льственный
магази́н; бакале́йная ла́вка
ground, земля́
group, гру́ппа
grow (intr.), расти́ (расту́, растёшь;
рос, росла́); tr. выра́щивать/
вы́растить (–ращу, –растишь)
gym, гимнасти́ческий зал

hair, во́лос, g.pl. воло́с
half, полови́на; — an hour, полчаса́
hall, пере́дняя
halt, остана́вливать/останови́ть
(остановлю́, остано́вишь);
остана́вливаться/останови́ться
ham, ветчина́
hand, рука́; on the one (the other) —,
с одно́й (друго́й) стороны́
handkerchief, (носово́й) плато́к,
платка́; dim. плато́чек, плато́чка
handsome, краси́вый, sht.fm. кра-
си́в, –а, –о; хоро́ш (хороша́)
собо́й
happen, случа́ться/–и́ться
happy, счастли́вый, sht.fm. сча́ст-
лив, –а, –ы
hard (difficult), тру́дный, sht.fm.
–ден, –дна́, –дно
hate, ненави́деть (–ви́жу, –ви́-
дишь)/воз–
have, use у + gen.; have to (must),
на́до, ну́жно, прихо́дится
(–ходи́лось/–шло́сь; –дётся)
+ dat.
he, он (его́, ему́, им, о нём)
head, голова́, acc. го́лову,
pl. го́ловы, голо́в
headache, головна́я боль; I have a
—, у меня́ боли́т голова́
hear, слы́шать (слы́шу, слы́-
шишь)/у–

heart, се́рдце, *pl.* –дца́, –де́ц; by —, наизу́сть

heat, жара́

heavy, тяжёлый, *sht.fm.* тяжёл, –а́, –о́

help, помога́ть/помо́чь (–могу́, –мо́жешь . . . –мо́гут; –мо́г, –могла́) + *dat.*; *n.* по́мощь *f.*

hen, ку́рица, *pl.* ку́ры

her, её; свой, –я́, –ё

herd, ста́до, *pl.* стада́, стад

here, здесь, тут; вот

heroic, герои́ческий

herself, see *self*

hide-and-seek, (игра́ в) пря́тки

high, высо́кий, *sht.fm.* высо́к, –а́, –о́

hill, холм

himself, see *self*

his, его́; свой, –я́, –ё

historic, historical, истори́ческий

history, исто́рия

hold, держа́ть (держу́, де́ржишь)/ по–; **be held** (take place), состо-я́ться (–сто́ится) *pfv.*

hole, дыра́

holiday, пра́здник; о́тпуск (в от пуску́), *pl.* –а́, –о́в; —**s**, кани́-кулы, кани́кул; о́тдых

holidaymaker, отдыха́ющий

Holland, Голла́ндия

home, домо́й; **at** —, до́ма

homework, дома́шняя рабо́та, дома́шнее зада́ние (*usu.* дома́ш ние зада́ния, *pl.*)

hoot, крича́ть (кричу́, кричи́шь)/ по–. за–, кри́кнуть (кри́кну, кри́кнешь)

hope, наде́яться (наде́юсь наде́-ешься)

horse, ло́шадь *f.*

hospitable, гостеприи́мный, *sht.fm.* –мен, –мна, –мно

hospital, больни́ца

hot, жа́ркий, *sht.fm.* –рок, –рка́, –рко

hotel, гости́ница

hour, час

house, дом, *pl.* –а́, –о́в; *dim.* до́мик

how, как

however, одна́ко; *conj.* как . . . ни

huge, грома́дный, *sht.fm.* –ден, –дна, –дно; огро́мный, *sht.fm.* –мен, –мна, –мно

hullo, здра́вствуй(те)

hundred, сто; **hundreds of**, со́тни, со́тен + *g.pl.*

hurry, спеши́ть/по–, торопи́ться (тороплю́сь, торо́пишься)/по–

I, я (меня́, мне, мной, о́бо мне)

ice-cream, моро́женое

ideal (*adj.*), идеа́льный, *sht.fm.* –лен, –льна, –льно

if, е́сли; (whether) ли

ill, больно́й, *sht.fm.* –лен, –льна́, –льно; **be** —, боле́ть (–е́ю, –е́ешь)/за–

illness, боле́знь *f.*

immediately, сра́зу (же), сейча́с (же), то́тчас (же)

impatient, нетерпели́вый, *sht.fm.* –ли́в, –а, –о

important, ва́жный, *sht.fm.* –жен, –жна́, –жно

improvement, улучше́ние

in, в (во) + *acc.*, + *prep.*; на + *prep.*; че́рез + *acc.*; **into**, в (во) + *acc.*

India, И́ндия

Indian, инди́йский

indoors, до́ма, внутри́ до́ма

interested, be, интересова́ться (–у́юсь, –у́ешься)/за– + *instr.*

interesting, интере́сный, *sht.fm.* –сен, –сна, –сно

interval, промежу́ток, проме-жу́тка; антра́кт

invite, приглаша́ть/пригласи́ть (–глашу́, –гласи́шь)

island, о́стров, *pl.* –а́, –о́в

it, оно́ (его́, ему́, им, о нём); он (see *he*); она́ (see *she*); э́то

Italy, Ита́лия

its, его́; её; свой, –я́, –ё

itself, see *self*

jacket, пиджа́к

January, янва́рь *m.*

join, присоединя́ть(ся)/–и́ть(ся) к + *dat.*

jolly, весёлый, *sht.fm.* ве́сел, –а́, –о

journey, путеше́ствие; пое́здка, *g.pl.* –док; **return** —, обра́тный путь (на обра́тном пути́)

jump down, соска́кивать/соскочи́ть

just, как раз; и́менно; ро́вно; сей-ча́с; **only** —, то́лько что; — **then**, и́менно тогда́, в ту са́мую мину́-ту; про́сто, то́лько

keep, держа́ть (держу́, де́ржишь)/по–; — **one's balance**, баланси́ровать (-ую, -уешь); — **up with**, держа́ться наравне́ с +*instr.*, не отстава́ть (–стаю́, –стаёшь)/отста́ть (–ста́ну, –ста́нешь) от +*gen.*
Kiev, Ки́ев
kind, до́брый, *sht.fm.* добр, –а́, –о
king, коро́ль, короля́
kiss, целова́ть (целу́ю, целу́ешь)/по–
kitchen, ку́хня
knee, коле́но, *pl.* –е́ни, –е́н
knit, вяза́ть (вяжу́, вя́жешь)/с–
knob, ру́чка, *g.pl.* –чек; кно́пка, *g.pl.* –пок
knock, стуча́ть (стучу́, стучи́шь)/по–, за–, сту́кнуть (сту́кну, сту́кнешь)
know, знать (узна́ть *pfv.*, get to know, find out)
known, изве́стный, *sht.fm.* –тен, –тна, –тно
Kolomna, Коло́мна
Kremlin, Кремль *m.*

laboratory, лаборато́рия
lady, да́ма
lake, о́зеро, *pl.* озёра, озёр
lamp, ла́мпа
land (of aircraft), приземля́ться/–ли́ться
language, язы́к
larder, кладова́я
large, большо́й, –а́я, –о́е, *sht.fm.* вели́к, –а́, –о; *comp.* бо́льше, бо́льший; *sup.* (са́мый) бо́льший
last, про́шлый; после́дний, –яя, –ее; **at** —, наконе́ц
late, по́здний, –яя, –ее; *adv.* по́здно; *comp.* поздне́е, по́зже; **to be** —, опа́здывать/опозда́ть на + *acc.*; **an hour later**, че́рез час; **latest**, нове́йший
lately, неда́вно; за после́днее вре́мя
laugh, смех; *vb.* смея́ться (смею́сь, смеёшься)/за–
lead, води́ть (вожу́, во́дишь)–вести́ (веду́, веде́шь; вёл, вела́)/повести́
leaf, лист, *pl.* –ья, –ьев

learn, учи́ться/вы–, на– + *dat.*
leave (home), выходи́ть (–хожу́, –хо́дишь)/вы́йти (–йду, –йдешь; –шел, –шла) (и́з дому); (of trains) отходи́ть/отойти́; (of planes) вылета́ть/–еть (–чу, –тишь)
left, ле́вый; *adv.* нале́во; **on the** —, сле́ва от +*gen.*
leg, нога́
legend, леге́нда
lemon, лимо́н
lemonade, лимона́д
Lenin Hills, Ле́нинские го́ры
Leningrad, Ленингра́д
lesson, уро́к; заня́тия, заня́тий, no *sg.*
let know, дава́ть (даю́, даёшь)/дать (дам, дашь, даст, дади́м, дади́те, даду́т) знать
letter, письмо́, *pl.* –сьма, –сем
library, библиоте́ка
lie, лежа́ть (лежу́, лежи́шь)/по–
life, жизнь *f.*
lift, give a, подвози́ть (–вожу́, –во́зишь)/подвезти́ (–везу́, –везёшь; –вёз, –везла́); довози́ть/довезти́
light, свет; *adj.* све́тлый, *sht.fm.* –тел, –тла́, –тло; *vb.* зажига́ть/заже́чь (–жгу́, –жжёшь . . . –жгу́т; –жёг, –жгла́); (cigarette) заку́ривать/закури́ть папиро́су
like, use нра́виться (нра́влюсь, нра́вишься)/ по– + *dat.*; люби́ть (люблю́, лю́бишь)/по–
like (*conj.*), как
listen, слу́шать/по– + *acc.*
little, ма́ленький, *sht.fm.* мал, –а́, –о́; *pron.* ма́ло + *gen.*; **a** —, немно́го, немно́жко + *gen.*
live, жить (живу́, живёшь)/по–, про–
locked, за́пертый, *sht.fm.* за́перт, –а́, –о
lonely, одино́кий, *sht.fm.* –о́к, –о́ка, –о́ко; малолю́дный
long, дли́нный, *sht.fm.* –нен, –нна́, –нно; до́лгий, *sht.fm.* –лог, –лга́, –лго; — **ago**, давно́; **a** — **way from**, далеко́ от +*gen.*
look, смотре́ть (смотрю́, смо́тришь)/по–; загля́дывать/загляну́ть; — **after**, смотре́ть/

70

по– за + *instr*.; — **for,** искáть
(–щý, –щешь); — **out** (overlook,
of windows etc.) выходúть в, на
+ *acc*.; *n.* взгляд
lorry, грузовúк
lose, теря́ть/по–; — **sight of,**
теря́ть/по– из вúду
lot, a, мнóго + *gen*.
love, любóвь, любвú; *vb.* любúть
(люблю́, лю́бишь)/по–
lovely, красúвый, *sht.fm*. –úв, –а, –о
low, нúзкий, *sht.fm*. –зок, –зкá,
–зко
luck, счáстье; **the best of —,** всегó
хорóшего (лýчшего, наилýч-
шего)
luckily, к счáстью
lucky, счастлúвый; **I am —,** мне
повезлó
luggage, багáж
lunch, зáвтрак; обéд; *vb.* зáвтра-
кать/по–; обéдать/по–

mad, сумасшéдший; (of a dog)
бéшеный
magazine, журнáл
magnificent, великолéпный, *sht.fm*
–пен, –пна, –пно
main, глáвный
make, дéлать/с–; (compel) застав-
ля́ть/застáвить (–стáвлю, –стá-
вишь)
man, мужчúна; (human being)
человéк, *pl.* лю́ди, людéй or
человéк *g.pl.*
manage, use удаётся, удавáлось/
удáстся, удалóсь) + *dat*.; (be in
time) успевáть/успéть (успéю,
успéешь)
many, мнóго + *g.pl*.; мнóгие; **how
—,** скóлько + *g.pl*.; **so —,** так
мнóго, стóлько
map, кáрта
March, март
market, ры́нок, ры́нка
massive, крýпный, *sht.fm*. –пен,
–пнá, –пно; массúвный, *sht.fm*.
–вен, –вна, –вно
master (teacher), учúтель, *pl.* –я́,
–éй; преподавáтель; (ruler)
хозя́ин, *pl.* хозя́ева, хозя́ев
match, спúчка, *g.pl*. –чек
mathematics, математика

matter, дéло, *pl.* делá, дел; **what is
the —,** в чём дéло
May, май
may, use мóжно + *dat*.
meadow, луг, *pl.* –á, –óв
mean, знáчить; хотéть (хочý,
хóчешь, хóчет, хотúм, хотúте,
хотя́т) сказáть
meat, мя́со
medicine, лекáрство
meet, встречáть/встрéтить
(встрéчу, встрéтишь); встре-
чáться/встрéтиться с + *instr*.
meeting, встрéча
member, член
mention, упоминáть/упомянýть
(упомяну́, упомя́нешь)
merchant, купéц, купцá
merely, тóлько, прóсто
Metro, метрó *indecl*.
midday, пóлдень; **by —,** к полýдню
middle, середúна; **in the — of,**
посередúне + *gen*.
mile, мúля
million, миллиóн
minute, минýта
miss, пропускáть/пропустúть
(–пущý, –пýстишь); опáзды-
вать/опоздáть на + *acc*.
mistake, ошúбка, *g.pl*. –бок
modern, совремéнный, *sht.fm*.
–нен, –ннá, –нно
moment, мгновéние, минýта; **just
a —,** одúн момéнт, однý минýту
Monday, понедéльник
money, дéньги, дéнег, *pl.* only
month, мéсяц, *g.pl*. –цев
monument, пáмятник
more, бóльше + *gen*.; (in comparatives) бóлее; **— and —,** всё бóльше; **— than once,** не раз; **once —,**
ещё раз
morning, ýтро; **in the —,** ýтром;
good —, дóброе ýтро; **next —,** на
другóе ýтро; **one —,** однáжды
ýтром; *adj.* ýтренний, –яя, –ее
Moscow, Москвá; *adj.* москóвский
Moskva, Москвá-рекá
most, большинствó, бóльшая
часть + *gen*.; (in superlatives)
сáмый, –ая, –ое
mother, мать, мáтери; (as form of
address) мáма
mountain, горá

71

move (of vehicles), ходи́ть (хожу́,
хо́дишь)–идти́ (иду́, идёшь;
шёл, шла)/пойти́; (move house)
переезжа́ть/перее́хать (–е́ду,
–е́дешь); — off, отправля́ться/
отпра́виться (–пра́влюсь, –пра́-
вишься) в путь
much, мно́го + gen.; (with compara-
tive) гора́здо
mud, грязь f.
muddy, гря́зный, sht.fm. –зен, –зна́,
–зно
multistoreyed, многоэта́жный
Muscovite, москви́ч, g.pl. –че́й
museum, музе́й, pl. –е́и, –е́ев
music, му́зыка; — room, музы-
ка́льный кабине́т
must, до́лжен, должна́, должны́;
на́до, ну́жно + dat.; (probably)
должно́ быть
my, мой, –я́, –ё; свой, –я́, –ё
myself, see self

name, и́мя, и́мени, pl. имена́, имён;
(surname) фами́лия
narrow, у́зкий, sht.fm. у́зок, узка́,
у́зко
near, бли́зко от + gen.; nearer,
бли́же к + dat.
nearby, вблизи́
nearly, почти́
necessary, ну́жный, sht.fm. ну́жен,
–жна́, –жно; необходи́мый,
–и́м, –и́ма, –и́мо
need, use ну́жен + dat., see necessary
neighbour, сосе́д, pl. –и, –ей
never, никогда́; — mind, ничего́,
нева́жно
new, но́вый, sht.fm. нов, –а́, –о
next, сле́дующий, –ая, –ее; сосе́д-
ний, –яя, –ее
nice, хоро́ший, –ая, –ее, sht.fm.
хоро́ш, –а́, –о́; сла́вный; прия́т-
ный, sht.fm. –тен, –тна, –тно
night, ночь f.; at —, но́чью
nine, де́вять; nineteen hundred and
forty-one, ты́сяча девятьсо́т
со́рок оди́н (пе́рвый); . . . and
forty-five, ... со́рок пять (пя́тый);
... and sixty, ... шестьдеся́т
(шестидеся́тый)
no, нет; adj. никако́й
nobody, no one, никто́

72

nod, кива́ть/кивну́ть (кивну́,
кивнёшь) + instr.
noise, шум; make —, шуме́ть
(–млю́, –ми́шь)/за–
noiseless, бесшу́мный, sht.fm.
–мен, –мна, –мно
noisy, шу́мный, sht.fm. –мен,
–мна́, –мно
none (pron.), никто́, ничто́; adj.
никако́й
north, се́вер; in the —, на се́вере;
adj. се́верный
northerly, see north (adj.)
not, не; is —, нет (не́ было, не
бу́дет) + gen.
notice, замеча́ть/заме́тить (–ме́чу,
–ме́тишь)
novel, рома́н
November, ноя́брь m.
now, тепе́рь, сейча́с; nowadays,
тепе́рь, в на́ше вре́мя
nowhere, нигде́; mtn. никуда́; with
infin. не́где, не́куда
numerous, многочи́сленный, sht.
fm. –ен, –енна, –енно

obviously, очеви́дно
occur, приходи́ть (–хо́дит)/прийти́
(–дёт; –шёл, –шла́) в го́лову +
dat.
o'clock, час (два часа́, пять часо́в)
October, октя́брь m.
of, от + gen.; из + gen.; о (об, о́бо)
+ prep.
offer, предлага́ть/предложи́ть
office, конто́ра
officer, офице́р
often, ча́сто; comp. ча́ще
old, ста́рый, sht.fm. стар, –а́, –о;
comp. ста́рше, ста́рший; sup.
(са́мый) ста́рший; — man,
стари́к
omelette, яи́чница, омле́т
on, на + acc.; о + prep.; по + dat.
once, раз; at —, сра́зу (же), сейча́с
(же), то́тчас (же); — more, ещё
раз, сно́ва
one, оди́н, одна́, одно́
only, то́лько, всего́
open, открыва́ть/откры́ть (–кро́ю,
–кро́ешь); p.p.p. откры́тый; in
the —, на откры́том во́здухе
opinion, мне́ние; in my —, по-мо́ему

opportunity, слу́чай, *pl.* –аи, –аев
or, и́ли; — **else**, ина́че, а то
orange, апельси́н
order, зака́зывать/заказа́ть
(–кажу́, –ка́жешь); **in — to**, (для
того́,) чтобы
other, друго́й; **the — day**, на днях
our, наш, –а, –е; свой, –я́, –ё
ourselves, see *self*
outskirts, окра́ина
over, над + *instr.*; (more than)
бо́льше, свы́ше + *gen.*; (finished)
use конча́ться/–иться
overcoat, пальто́ *indecl.*
overcrowded, перепо́лненный, *sht.*
fm. –нен, –нена, –нено
owl, сова́
own, со́бственный; **on his —**, сам,
–а́, –и; оди́н, одна́, одни́

pack, укла́дывать/уложи́ть
pair, па́ра
palace, дворе́ц, дворца́
paper, бума́га; (newspaper) газе́та
parents, роди́тели, роди́телей
park, парк
part, часть *f.*
particularly, осо́бенно
partisan, партиза́н, *g.pl.* партиза́н;
— **detachment**, партиза́нский
отря́д
pass, проходи́ть (–хожу́, –хо́дишь)/
пройти́ (–йду́, –йдёшь; –шёл,
–шла́) ми́мо + *gen.*
passage, прохо́д, коридо́р
passenger, пассажи́р; *adj.* пасса-
жи́рский
passport, па́спорт, *pl.* –а́, –о́в
past (last), про́шлый; после́дний,
–яя, –ее; (at) **half past nine**, поло-
ви́на (в полови́ну ог полови́не)
деся́того
path, тропи́нка, *g.pl.* –нок;
доро́жка, *g.pl.* –жек
pavement, тротуа́р
pay, плати́ть (плачу́, пла́тишь)/
за– за + *acc.*
peas, горо́х, no *pl.*
pear, гру́ша
peasant girl, (де́вушка-) кресть-
я́нка, *g.pl.* –нок
peninsula, полуо́стров
people, лю́ди, люде́й

perceptible, заме́тный, *sht.fm.* –тен,
–тна, –тно
perhaps, мо́жет быть
perilous, опа́сный, *sht.fm.* –сен,
–сна, –сно
period, эпо́ха
person, челове́к, *pl.* лю́ди, люде́й
ог челове́к
physics, фи́зика
pick up, поднима́ть/подня́ть
(–ниму́, –ни́мешь); захва́ты-
вать/захвати́ть (–хвачу́, –хва́-
тишь); брать (беру́, берёшь)/
взять (возьму́, возьмёшь)
picture, карти́на
picturesque, живопи́сный, *sht.fm.*
–сен, –сна, –сно
pillow, поду́шка, *g.pl.* –шек
pioneer, пионе́р; *adj.* пионе́рский
pipe, тру́бка, *g.pl.* –бок
pity, it's a, (о́чень) жаль, что
place, ме́сто, *pl.* места́, мест
plain, просто́й, *sht.fm.* прост, –а́, –о
plan, план; **make —s**, стро́ить/по-
пла́ны
plane, самолёт
plate, таре́лка, *g.pl.* –лок
platform, платфо́рма, перро́н
play, пье́са; *vb.* игра́ть/сыгра́ть,
по–
pleasant, прия́тный, *sht.fm.* –тен,
–тна, –тно
please, пожа́луйста
pleased, дово́лен, –льна, –льны +
instr.
plenty of, мно́го + *gen.*
pocket, карма́н; — **money**, карма́н-
ные де́ньги
poem, стихотворе́ние; стихи́, –о́в
(*coll.*)
point to, ука́зывать/указа́ть
(–кажу́, –ка́жешь) на + *acc.*
Poland, По́льша
Polish, по́льский
poor, бе́дный, *sht.fm.* –ден, –дна́,
–дно
popular, популя́рный, *sht.fm.* –рен,
–рна, –рно; люби́мый
population, населе́ние
portrait, портре́т
poster, плака́т
potatoes, карто́фель *m.*, no *pl.*
powerful, могу́чий, *sht.fm.* –у́ч,
–а, –е

73

prepare (*refl.*), гото́виться (–влюсь, –вишься)/при– к + *dat.*
prepared, гото́вый, *sht.fm.* гото́в, –а, –о
pretty, краси́вый, *sht.fm.* –и́в, –и́ва, –и́во; хоро́шенький, *sht.fm.* хоро́ш, –á, –ó (собо́й)
previous, предыду́щий, –ая, –ее; **on the — day**, накану́не
price, цена́
prisoner, пле́нник; **take —**, брать (беру́, берёшь)/взять (возьму́, возьмёшь) в плен
promise, обеща́ть
proud, го́рдый, *sht.fm.* горд, –á, –о + *instr.*; **be —**, горди́ться (горжу́сь, горди́шься) + *instr.*
Prussia, Пру́ссия
pupil, учени́к; *fem.* учени́ца
purchase, поку́пка, *g.pl.* –пок
pure, чи́стый, *sht.fm.* чист, –á, –о
put (standing), ста́вить (ста́влю, ста́вишь)/по–; (lay) класть (кладу́, кладёшь; клал, кла́ла)/положи́ть; **— on**, надева́ть/наде́ть –де́ну, –де́нешь)

quarter, че́тверть *f.*
queen, короле́ва
question, вопро́с; **ask a —**, задава́ть/зада́ть вопро́с
queue, о́чередь *f.*; **go and —**, станови́ться (становлю́сь, стано́вишься)/стать (ста́ну, ста́нешь) в о́чередь; **be —ing**, стоя́ть (стою́, стои́шь)/по– в о́череди
quick, бы́стрый, *sht.fm.* быстр, –á, –о; **as quickly as possible**, как мо́жно быстре́е
quiet, ти́хий, *sht.fm.* тих, –á, –о; *comp.* ти́ше
quite, совсе́м; (fairly) дово́льно

rabbit, кро́лик
radio, ра́дио *indecl.*; радиоприёмник; радиоте́хника; **— amateur**, радиолюби́тель
railway, желе́зная доро́га; **— track**, железнодоро́жная колея́
rain, дождь *m.*; **it is —ing**, дождь идёт
rainy, дождли́вый, *sht.fm.* –и́в, –и́ва, –и́во

raise, поднима́ть/подня́ть (–ниму́, –ни́мешь)
range, цепь, *f.*
rarely, ре́дко; *comp.* ре́же
rather, дово́льно
reach, доходи́ть (–хожу́, –хо́дишь)/дойти́ (–йду́, –йдёшь; –шёл, –шла́); добира́ться/добра́ться (–беру́сь, –берёшься) до + *gen.*
read, чита́ть/про–
reading, чте́ние
ready, гото́вый, *sht.fm.* –о́в, –а, –о; **to get —**, собира́ться/собра́ться (–беру́сь, –берёшься)
realise, понима́ть/поня́ть (–иму́, –и́мёшь)
really, действи́тельно, в са́мом де́ле
rear, за́дний, –яя, –ее; **at the —**, позади́, сза́ди
receive, получа́ть/–и́ть
recently, неда́вно; за после́днее вре́мя
recognise, узнава́ть (узнаю́, узнаёшь)/узна́ть
recreation, о́тдых
red, кра́сный
refuse, отка́зываться/отказа́ться (–кажу́сь, –ка́жешься) от + *gen.*
region, страна́; край, *pl.* –я́, –ёв
relax, отдыха́ть/отдохну́ть
reliable, надёжный, *sht.fm.* –жен, –жна, –жно
remarkable, замеча́тельный, *sht. fm.* –лен, –льна, –льно
remember, по́мнить/за–; вспомина́ть/вспо́мнить
remind, напомина́ть/напо́мнить + *dat.*
reply, отве́т; *vb.* отвеча́ть/отве́тить (–ве́чу, –ве́тишь) + *dat.* (на вопро́с)
residence, резиде́нция
resolve, реша́ть(ся)/–и́ть(ся)
resort, куро́рт (на куро́рте)
rest home, дом о́тдыха
restaurant, рестора́н
result, результа́т
return, возвраща́ться/верну́ться (верну́сь, вернёшься)
revolution, револю́ция
ride, е́здить (е́зжу, е́здишь)–е́хать (е́ду, е́дешь)/пое́хать верхо́м
right, пра́вый, *sht.fm.* прав, –á, –о;

on the —, спра́ва от +*gen.*; —
away, сра́зу же; — **in, on**, etc., use
  са́мый, –ая, –ое
ring, звони́ть/по–
rise, встава́ть (встаю́, встаёшь)/
  встать (вста́ну, вста́нешь); под-
  нима́ться/подня́ться (–ниму́сь,
  –ни́мешься)
river, река́; *dim.* ре́чка, *g.pl.* –чек
road, доро́га; у́лица
rock, скала́
roof, кры́ша
room, ко́мната; (space) ме́сто
rose, ро́за
round, кру́глый, *sht.fm.* кругл, –ла́,
  –ло
row, ряд, *pl.* –ды́, –о́в
rule, пра́вило; **as a —**, как пра́вило
run, бе́гать–бежа́ть (бегу́, бежи́шь
  . . . бегу́т)/побежа́ть; (buses, etc.)
  ходи́ть (хожу́, хо́дишь)–идти́
  (иду́, идёшь; шёл, шла)/пойти́;
  — up to, подбега́ть/подбежа́ть
  (–гу́, –жи́шь . . . –гу́т) к +*dat.*
rush hour, часы́ пик
Russia, Росси́я; Сове́тский Сою́з
Russian (*n.* and *adj.*), ру́сский
rustle, шуме́ть (шумлю́, шуми́шь)/
  по–, за–; шелесте́ть (шелести́т)/
  за– +*instr.*

sack, мешо́к, мешка́
same, тот же (са́мый); оди́н, одна́,
  одно́
sanatorium, санато́рий, *pl.* –ии,
  –иев
sandwich, бутербро́д; сэ́ндвич,
  g.pl. –ей
sandy, песча́ный
Saratov, Сара́тов
Saturday, суббо́та
save (up), нака́пливать/накопи́ть
  (–коплю́, –ко́пишь)
say, говори́ть/сказа́ть (скажу́,
  ска́жешь)
scarcely, едва́ (ли)
scarf, плато́к, платка́
school, шко́ла; **primary —**, нача́ль-
  ная шко́ла; **secondary —**, сре́д-
  няя шко́ла; **—boy**, шко́льник;
  — friend, шко́льный това́рищ,
  това́рищ по шко́ле; *adj.* шко́ль-
  ный
Scotland, Шотла́ндия

Scythian, скиф
sea, мо́ре, *pl.* –я́, –е́й
seaside, to (at) the, на мо́ре, на
  бе́рег (берегу́) мо́ря; *adj.* при-
  мо́рский
season, вре́мя (вре́мени, *pl.* вре-
  мена́, времён) го́да
seat, ме́сто, *pl.* места́, мест;
  сиде́ние
second, второ́й
see, ви́деть (ви́жу, ви́дешь)/у–
seem, каза́ться (ка́жется)/по–
self (*refl.*), себя́ (себе́, собо́й, о
  себе́); *emph.pron.* сам, –а́, –о́,
  pl. –и
sell, продава́ть (–даю́, –даёшь)/
  прода́ть (–да́м, –да́шь, –да́ст,
  –дади́м, –дади́те, –даду́т)
September, сентя́брь *m.*
Sergei, Серге́й (Серёжа)
serious, серьёзный, *sht.fm.* –зен,
  –зна, –зно
serve, служи́ть/по– +*dat.*; обслу́-
  живать/обслужи́ть +*acc.*
set off, отправля́ться/отпра́виться
  (–пра́влюсь, –пра́вишься) в путь
seven, семь; **seventeen hundred and
  eighty-nine**, ты́сяча семьсо́т
  во́семьдесят во́семь (восьмо́й)
seven-year school, (шко́ла–)семи-
  ле́тка, семиле́тняя шко́ла
several, не́сколько +*g.pl.*
severe, суро́вый, *sht.fm.* –о́в, –о́ва,
  –о́во
shake hands, пожима́ть/пожа́ть
  (–жму́, –жмёшь) ру́ку +*dat.*
sharp, о́стрый, *sht.fm.* остр, –а́, –о;
  ре́зкий, *sht.fm.* –зок, –зка́, –зко
she, она́ (её, ей, о ней)
sheep, овца́, *pl.* о́вцы, ове́ц
sheet, простыня́, *pl.* про́стыни,
  просты́нь
shelf, по́лка, *g. pl.* –лок
shine, сия́ть (сия́ю, сия́ешь)/за–
shirt, руба́шка, *pl.* –шек
shoes, ту́фли, ту́фель; боти́нки,
  –нок
shoot (dead), застре́ливать/за-
  стреля́ть
shop, магази́н; ла́вка, *g. pl.* –вок
shopkeeper, ла́вочник
shopper, покупа́тель
shopping, do some, де́лать/с– по-
  ку́пки; ходи́ть (хожу́, хо́дишь)–

идти́ (иду́, идёшь; шёл, шла)/
пойти́ за поку́пками; **shopping
bag**, су́мка (*g.pl.* –мок) для
поку́пок
shore, бе́рег (на берегу́), *pl.* –а́, –о́в
short, коро́ткий, *sht.fm.* –ток, тка́,
–тко; *comp.* коро́че
shout, крича́ть (кричу́, крич–ь)/
по–, за–, кри́кнуть (кри́и́шкну,
кри́кнешь)
show, пока́зывать/показа́ть
(–кажу́, –ка́жешь) + *dat.*
shrub, куст
side, сторона́; бок, *pl.* –а́, –о́в;
— **street**, переу́лок, переу́лка;
бокова́я у́лица
sigh, вздыха́ть/вздохну́ть; *n.* вздох
sight, уви́деть (уви́жу, уви́дишь)
pfv.
sign, знак, при́знак
silence, in, мо́лча
silent, be, молча́ть (молчу́, мол-
чи́шь)/по–, за–; *adj.* ти́хий, *sht.
fm.* тих, –а́, –о
silly, глу́пый, *sht.fm.* глуп, –а́, –о
similar, похо́жий, –ая, –ее, *sht.fm.*
похо́ж, –а, –е, на + *acc.*
simple, просто́й, *sht.fm.* прост,
–а́, –о
since (*prp.*), с (со) + *gen.*; *conj.*
с тех пор, как; *adv.* с тех пор
sing, петь (пою́, поёшь)/с–, за-
single, not a, use ни оди́н (одна́,
одно́)
sister, сестра́, *pl.* сёстры, сестёр;
dim. сестри́ца
sit, сиде́ть (сижу́, сиди́шь)/по-
sitting-room, гости́ная
situated, располо́женный, *sht.fm.*
–жен, –а, –о
six, шесть; **sixty**, шестьдеся́т
sky, не́бо
skyscraper, небоскрёб; высо́тный
дом (*pl.* –а́, –о́в)
sleep, спать (сплю, спишь)/по-
sleeping-car, спа́льный ваго́н
sleeve, рука́в, *pl.* –а́, –о́в
slippery, ско́льзкий, *sht.fm.* –зок,
–зька́, –зько
slow, ме́дленный, *sht.fm.* –лен,
–ленна, –ленно
small, ма́ленький, *sht.fm.* мал, –а́,
–о́; *comp.* ме́ньше, ме́ньший;
sup. (са́мый) ме́ньший

smile, улы́бка; *vb.* улыба́ться/
улыбну́ться (улыбну́сь, улыб-
нёшься)
smoke, кури́ть/по–, за–
Smolensk, Смоле́нск
snow, снег; **it is —ing**, снег идёт
snowdrift, (снéжный) сугро́б
snowstorm, метéль *f.*
so, так; **and — on**, и так да́лее
sock, носо́к, носка́
sofa, дива́н
soft, мя́гкий, *sht.fm.* мя́гок, –гка́,
–гко
solemn, торже́ственный, *sht.fm.*
–вен, –венна, –венно
solitary, одино́кий, *sht.fm.* –о́к,
–о́ка, –о́ко
some (a little), немно́го + *g.sg.*;
(a few) не́сколько + *g.pl.*; or use
part.gen.; —**how**, ка́к-то, ка́к-
нибудь; —**thing**, что́-то, что́-
нибудь; —**time**, когда́-то, когда́-
нибудь; —**times**, иногда́; —
where, где́-то, где́-нибудь; *mtn.*
куда́-то, куда́-нибудь
son, сын, *pl.* сыновья́, сынове́й
soon, ско́ро; —**er**, ра́ньше; **as — as
possible**, как мо́жно скоре́е
sorry, I am, извини́(те); винова́т,
–а; **I feel — for**, мне жаль
(жа́лко) + *acc.*
sound, звук; шум
south, юг; **in the —**, на ю́ге
southern, ю́жный
Soviet Union, Сове́тский Сою́з
Spain, Испа́ния
spare, ли́шний, –яя, –ее; свобо́д-
ный, *sht.fm.* –ден, –дна, –дно
speak, говори́ть/по-
special, осо́бенный; *adv.* осо́бенно
специа́льный, *sht.fm.* –лен,
–льна, –льно
spend (time), проводи́ть (–вожу́,
–во́дишь)/провести́ (–веду́,
–ведёшь; –вёл, –вела́) вре́мя;
— **night**, ночева́ть (–у́ю, –у́ешь)/
пере-
spoil, по́ртить (по́рчу, по́ртишь)/
ис-
spring, весна́; **in —**, весно́й
square, пло́щадь *f.*
squirrel, бе́лка, *g.pl.* –лок
stable, коню́шня, *g.pl.* –шен
stall, ларь, ларя́; ларёк, ларька́

stamp, ма́рка, *g.pl.* –рок
stand, стоя́ть (стою́, стои́шь)/по–;
— **up**, встава́ть (встаю́, встаёшь)/встать (вста́ну, вста́нешь)
start, начина́ть/нача́ть (начну́,
начнёшь); начина́ться/нача́ть-
ся; (of train, etc.) тро́гаться/тро́-
нуться (тро́нусь, тро́нешься)
state, госуда́рство
statesman, госуда́рственный
де́ятель
station, вокза́л; ста́нция; (radio)
радиоста́нция
stay, остава́ться (остаю́сь, оста-
ёшься)/оста́ться (оста́нусь,
оста́нешься); (live) жить (живу́,
живёшь)/по–, про–; (visit) гос-
ти́ть (гощу́, гости́шь)/по–
steady (of look, etc.), при́стальный,
sht.fm. –лен, –льна, –льно
steamer, парохо́д; *dim.* парохо́дик
step, шаг (два шага́)
steppe, степь *f.* (в степи́)
still (*adj.*), споко́йный, *sht.fm.* –6ен,
–о́йна, –о́йно; *adv.* (всё) ещё
stone, ка́мень, ка́мня; *adj.* ка́мен-
ный
stop, остана́вливать/останови́ть
(остановлю́, остано́вишь);
остана́вливаться/останови́ться
storey, эта́ж, *g.pl.* –е́й
story, расска́з
straight, прямо́й; *adv.* пря́мо; —
away, сра́зу же, сейча́с же, то́т-
час же
strange, стра́нный, *sht.fm.* –нен,
–нна́, –нно
stranger, незнако́мец, незнако́мца,
g.pl. –цев
street, у́лица
stretch (expanse), просто́р, про-
стра́нство
strike, поража́ть/порази́ть (–ражу́,
–рази́шь)
strong, си́льный, *sht.fm.* –лен
(–лён), –льна́, –льно
study, изуча́ть/–и́ть
stupid, глу́пый, *sht.fm.* глуп, –а́, –о
subject, предме́т
subtropical, субтропи́ческий
suburb, при́город
such, тако́й; так
suddenly, вдруг, внеза́пно
sugar, са́хар, *part.gen.* са́хару

suggest, предлага́ть/предложи́ть
suitable, удо́бный, *sht.fm.* –бен,
–бна, –бно
suitcase, чемода́н; *dim.* чемода́нчик
summer, ле́то; **in** —, ле́том
sun, со́лнце
sunbathe, лежа́ть (лежу́, лежи́шь)/
по– на со́лнце; загора́ть/за-
горе́ть (–горю́, –гори́шь)
Sunday, воскресе́нье
sunny, со́лнечный, *sht.fm.* –чен,
–чна, –чно
suntanned, загоре́лый
suppose, I, вероя́тно, должно́ быть
sure, уве́ренный, *sht.fm.* –ен, –ена
surely, ра́зве, неуже́ли
surprise, удивле́ние; **to my** —, к
моему́ (своему́) уливле́нию; **to
be surprised**, удивля́ться/удиви́-
ться (удивлю́сь, удиви́шься)
+ *dat.*
surroundings, окре́стности, *pl.* only
swim, пла́вать–плыть (плыву́,
плывёшь)/поплы́ть
switch on, включа́ть/–и́ть
symbol, си́мвол
system, систе́ма

table, стол; *dim.* сто́лик
take, брать (беру́, берёшь)/взять
(возьму́, возьмёшь); — **off** (of
aircraft) взлета́ть/взлете́ть
(–лечу́, –лети́шь), отрыва́ться/
оторва́ться (–рву́сь, –рвёшься)
от земли́; — **out**, вынима́ть/
вы́нуть (–ну, –нешь) из +*gen.*;
— **part**, принима́ть/приня́ть
(–му́, –мешь) уча́стие, уча́ство-
вать (уча́ствую, уча́ствуешь)
в +*prep.*; — **someone to be**, при-
нима́ть/приня́ть кого́-нибудь
за +*acc.*
taken (occupied), за́нятый, *sht.fm.*
–ят, –а́, –о
talk, говори́ть/по–; разгова́ривать
tall, высо́кий, *sht.fm.* высо́к, –а́,
–о́; *comp.* вы́ше
Tanya, Та́ня (Татья́на)
Tauris, Таври́да
taxi, такси́ *indecl.*
tea, чай, *part.gen.* ча́ю; **have** —,
пить (пью, пьёшь)/вы́– чай
teach, учи́ть/на– + *dat.* of subject

77

taught; преподава́ть (–даю́,
–даёшь) + *dat.* of persons taught
teacher, учи́тель, *pl.* –я́, –е́й, *fem.*
учи́тельница; преподава́тель,
fem. преподава́тельница
team, кома́нда
tear off, отрыва́ть/оторва́ть (–рву́,
–рвёшь)
tell, говори́ть/сказа́ть (скажу́,
ска́жешь); расска́зывать/рас-
сказа́ть
temperature, температу́ра; **to take
the —**, смеря́ть/–ить темпера-
ту́ру
ten, де́сять
tennis, те́ннис
terrible, ужа́сный, *sht.fm.* –сен,
–сна, –сно
Thames, (река́) Те́мза
than, чем
thank, благодари́ть/по– за + *acc.*;
thank you, thanks, спаси́бо за +
acc.; **many thanks**, большо́е спа-
си́бо
that, что; кото́рый; тот (та, то, те)
thaw, о́ттепель *f.*
theatre, теа́тр
their, их; свой, –я́, –ё
themselves, see *self*
then, тогда́; (afterwards) пото́м,
зате́м
there, там; вот; *mtn.* туда́; **from —**,
отту́да
therefore, поэ́тому
they, они́ (их, им, и́ми, о них)
thick, то́лстый, *sht.fm.* толст, –а́,
–о; (dense) густо́й, *sht.fm.* густ,
–а́, –о
thin, то́нкий, *sht.fm.* то́нок, –нка́,
–нко; худо́й, *sht.fm.* худ, –а́, –о
thing, вещь *f.*
think, ду́мать/по–; **I —**, мне ка́-
жется
thirteen, трина́дцать; **thirty**, три́д-
цать; **thirty-four**, три́дцать
четы́ре
this, э́тот (э́та, э́то, э́ти)
thousand, ты́сяча
three, три, тро́е; **— and a half**, три
(тро́е) с полови́ной
through, сквозь, че́рез + *acc.*
ticket, биле́т
time, вре́мя, вре́мени, *pl.* времена́,
времён; раз; **have a good —**,

хорошо́ проводи́ть (–вожу́,
–во́дишь)/провести́ (–веду́,
–ведёшь; –вёл, –вела́) вре́мя;
have —, успева́ть/успе́ть (–е́ю,
–е́ешь); **in —**, во́время; **it is —**,
пора́ + *infin.*
tired, уста́лый, *sht.fm.* уста́л, –а, –о
to, в (во), на + *acc.*, к (ко) + *dat.*
tobacco, таба́к; **— field**, таба́чное
по́ле (*pl.* –я́, –е́й)
today, сего́дня
together, вме́сте
Tolstoy, Leo, Лев Никола́евич
Толсто́й
tomato, помидо́р
too, сли́шком; (also) то́же, та́кже, и
towards, к (ко) + *dat.*
town, го́род, *pl.* –а́, –о́в; *dim.* горо-
до́к, городка́
tractor, тра́ктор
trade, торгова́ть (торгу́ю, тор-
гу́ешь)/по–
traditional, традицио́нный, *sht.fm.*
–нен, –нна, –нно
train, по́езд, *pl.* –а́, –о́в
tram, трамва́й, *pl.* –а́и, –а́ев
transmitter, (ра́дио–)переда́тчик
transport, тра́нспорт
travel, е́здить (е́зжу, е́здишь)–
е́хать (е́ду, е́дешь)/пое́хать;
путеше́ствовать (путеше́ствую,
путеше́ствуешь)
tree, де́рево, *pl.* дере́вья, –ьев
trip, пое́здка, *g.pl.* –док; прогу́лка,
g.pl. –лок; (plane) полёт; **go for a
—**, де́лать/с– (соверша́ть/–и́ть)
пое́здку, прогу́лку
trolley-bus, тролле́йбус
trouble, беда́; **the — is**, беда́ в том
trousers, брю́ки, брюк
true, it is, пра́вда; **not —**, непра́вда
truth, пра́вда
try, стара́ться/по–
tube, метро́ *indecl.*, метрополите́н
Tuesday, вто́рник
Turkey, Ту́рция
turn, о́чередь *f.*; *vb.* (*tr.*) верте́ть
(верчу́, ве́ртишь)/по–; крути́ть
(кручу́, кру́тишь)/по–; (*intr.*)
повора́чивать/поверну́ть (–вер-
ну́, –вернёшь); **— out to be**, ока́-
зываться/оказа́ться (–жу́сь,
–жешься) + *instr.*; **— round**, обо-
ра́чиваться/оберну́ться; **— to**

(address), обраща́ться/обрати́ться (обращу́сь, обрати́шься) к + *dat.*

twenty, два́дцать; **twenty-three**, два́дцать три (тре́тий, –ья, –ье); **twenty-four**, два́дцать четы́ре (четвёртый)

two, два, две *f.*; дво́е; **two-storeyed**, двухэта́жный

typical, типи́чный, *sht.fm.* –чен, –чно, –чно

uncle, дя́дя

under, под + *instr.*

underground, подзе́мный; *n.* see *tube*

understand, понима́ть/поня́ть (–йму́, –ймёшь)

unfortunately, к сожале́нию

university, университе́т

unshaven, небри́тый, *sht.fm.* небри́т

unsteady, ша́ткий, *sht.fm.* –ток, –тка, –ткс, нетвёрдый, *sht.fm.* нетвёрд, –да́, –до

until, пока́ . . . не + *pfv.vb.*

unusual, необыкнове́нный, *sht.fm.* –нен, –нна, –нно; необы́чный, *sht.fm.* –чен, –чна, –чно

up and down, взад и вперёд

upstairs, наверху́; *mtn.* наве́рх

use, по́льзоваться (–уюсь, –уешься)/вос– + *instr.*

useful, поле́зный, *sht.fm.* –зен, –зна, –зно

U.S.S.R., СССР (Сою́з Сове́тских Социалисти́ческих Респу́блик)

usual, обыкнове́нный, *sht.fm.* –нен, –нна, –нно; обы́чный, *sht.fm.* –чен, –чна, –чно

utterly, соверше́нно, абсолю́тно

vanish, исчеза́ть/исче́знуть (исче́зну, исче́знешь; исче́з, –ла)

vegetables, о́вощи, овоще́й

vehicle, маши́на

very, о́чень

view, вид

village, село́, *pl.* сёла, сёл; дере́вня, *g.pl.* дереве́нь

vineyard, виногра́дник

visa, ви́за

visit, заходи́ть (–хожу́, –хо́дишь)/зайти́ (–йду́, –йдёшь; –шёл, –шла́), заезжа́ть/зае́хать (–е́ду, –е́дешь) к + *dat.*; посеща́ть/посети́ть (–сещу́, –сети́шь)

visitor, посети́тель *m.*, гость *m.*

voice, го́лос, *pl.* –а́, –о́в

Volga, Во́лга

volleyball, волейбо́л

Volodya, Воло́дя (Влади́мир)

Voskresensk, Воскресе́нск

wait, ждать (жду, ждёшь)/подо– + *acc.* or *gen.*

waiter, официа́нт

waiting-room, приёмная

wake up (*tr.*), буди́ть (бужу́, бу́дишь)/раз–; (*intr.*) просыпа́ться/просну́ться (–сну́сь, –снёшься)

walk, прогу́лка, *pl.* –лок; ходьба́; *vb.* ходи́ть (хожу́, хо́дишь)–идти́ (иду́, идёшь; шёл, шла)/пойти́; гуля́ть/по–; — **up to**, подходи́ть/подойти́ к + *dat.*

wall, стена́, *pl.* сте́ны, стен

want, хоте́ть (хочу́, хо́чешь, хо́чет, хоти́м, хоти́те, хотя́т)/за–

war, война́

wardrobe, шкаф (в шкафу́)

warm, тёплый; *sht.fm.* тёпел, –пла́, –пло́

wash, мыть (мо́ю, мо́ешь)/вы́–; **have a —**, мы́ться/вы́мыться

watch, часы́, часо́в; *vb.* смотре́ть (смотрю́, смо́тришь)/по–

water, вода́, *acc.* во́ду

way, путь *m.*; доро́га; **by the —**, ме́жду про́чим; **on the — back**, на обра́тном пути́

we, мы (нас, нам, на́ми, о нас)

wear, носи́ть (ношу́, но́сишь); **be—ing**, use быть в + *prep.*, на + *prep.*

weather, пого́да

Wednesday, среда́

week, неде́ля; **this —**, на э́той неде́ле

well, хорошо́; **Well?** Ну?

wet, мо́крый, *sht.fm.* мокр, –а́, –о

what, что

wheel, колесо́, *n.pl.* колёса

when, когда́; **whenever**, (вся́кий раз), когда́

where, где; *mtn.* куда
whether, ли
which, какой; который
while, пока + *impfv.* vb.; a little —
  ago, недавно
whistle, свистеть (свищу, свистишь)/по–, свистнуть (свистну, свистнешь)
white, белый
White Guard officer, офицер-белогвардеец (–дейца)
who, кто; *rel.* который
whole, целый, *sht.fm.* цел, –а, –о
why, почему; отчего; зачем
wide, широкий, *sht.fm.* широк, –а, –о; *comp.* шире
wife, жена, *pl.* жёны, жён
win, выигрывать/выиграть
wind, ветер, ветра
window, окно, *pl.* окна, окон
winter, зима; in —, зимой; *adj.* зимний, –яя, –ее
wireless set, радио *indecl.*, радиоаппарат (–приёмник)
wish, желание, пожелание; *vb.* желать/по– + *gen.*
with, с (со) + *instr.*
without, без + *gen.*
wolf, волк
woman, женщина
wonder, спрашивать себя
wonderful, чудный, *sht.fm.* –ден, –дна, –дно

wood, лес (в лесу), *pl.* –а, –ов
wooden, деревянный
word, слово, *pl.* слова, слов; in a —, одним словом
work, работа; *vb.* работать/по–; действовать (–ую, –уешь)/по–; — out, вырабатывать/выработать
world, мир; *adj.* мировой
worry, беспокоиться/о–
wound, рана
write, писать (пишу, пишешь)/на–; writer, писатель
wrong, неправильный, *sht.fm.* –лен, –льна, –льно; не тот (не та, не то, не те)

yard, двор
year, год; this —, в этом году; — after —, из года в год
yes, да
yet, ещё; уже; not —, ещё не (нет)
you, ты (тебя, тебе, тобой, о тебе); вы (вас, вам, вами, о вас)
young, молодой, *sht.fm.* молод, –а, –о; *comp.* моложе, младший; *sup.* (самый) младший
your, твой, –я, –ё; ваш, –а, –е; свой, –я, –ё
yourself, see *self*
youth, молодость *f.*
Yury, Юрий; — Dolgoruky, Юрий Долгорукий